CHANGING ROLES

DUKE CORPORATE EDUCATION

CHANGING ROLES
ROLES
AVOIDING THE TRANSITION TRAPS

Blair Sheppard • Michael Canning
Marla Tuchinsky • Cindy Campbell

KAPLAN PUBLISHING

President, Kaplan Publishing: Roy Lipner
Vice President and Publisher: Maureen McMahon
Acquisitions Editor: Michael Cunningham
Development Editor: Trey Thoelcke
Production Editor: Karen Goodfriend
Typesetter: Janet Schroeder
Cover Designer: Design Solutions

Published by Kaplan Publishing,
a division of Kaplan, Inc.

Printed in the United States of America

06 07 08   10 9 8 7 6 5 4 3 2

Library of Congress Cataloging-in-Publication Data

Changing roles : avoiding the transition traps / Duke Corporate Education.
    p. cm.
  Includes bibliographical references and index.
  ISBN-13: 978-1-4195-3549-9 (alk. paper)
  ISBN-10: 1-4195-3549-8 (alk. paper)
  1. Career development. 2. Organizational change. 3. Career changes. 4. Adaptability (Psychology) I. Duke Corporate Education.
  HF5381.C44 2006
  650.1–dc22
                        2006008085

CONTENTS

ACKNOWLEDGMENTS

First and foremost, we continue to thank our clients and the many program participants around the globe. We begin our work by listening to our clients and gaining an understanding of their business challenges. Working with talented clients and actively engaging in their challenges across a range of industries and geographies has afforded us the opportunity to learn and develop an informed point of view on these topics. We thank our clients for trusting in our approach and making us part of their teams. They have shared their experiences and challenges and discussed at length the skills, tools, and mindsets covered in this book, thereby deepening our knowledge and insight.

We are also fortunate to have an extensive network of faculty, coaches, facilitators, and partners who believe in our mission and have opted to join in our adventure. Together, we have delivered programs in 43 different countries since we formed in July 2000. We absolutely could not have accomplished what we have and learned what we know without their collaboration.

Ryan Stevens again worked to help capture our methods and processes into the graphics included within the book, often working with vague instructions. As usual, he did a wonderful job.

Special thanks to Duke Corporate Education executive director John Malitoris and managing director Nancy Keeshan, who helped guide our thinking as we explored this topic. They read through the many drafts we produced, and their insights and feedback were always on target.

Perhaps more so than any of the other topics we have explored while writing the *Leading from the Center* series, the challenge of changing roles and the accompanying transition traps resonated strongly with many people. As we spoke with colleagues, clients, and friends, many responded by sharing both personal experiences and the experiences of others that they have observed as managers. We especially thank Bob Fulmer, Kirby Warren, Leah Houde, Bill Big-oness, Greg Marchi, Cheryl Stokes, Jane Kasper, George Penn, Car-rie Painter, and Steve Mahaley for their contributions.

As always, we could not have accomplished this without the guidance and assistance of our CEO, Blair Sheppard. He supported this initiative from the outset and, more importantly, always made time to review our output and guide our thinking. His assistance is without measure. We could not have done it without him.

We've drawn upon the insight, experience, and expertise from numerous colleagues here at Duke Corporate Education. We hope that the content of this book stimulates your thinking and improves your ability to navigate the transition process.

The *Changing Roles* team: Michael Canning, Marla Tuchinsky, Cindy Campbell, and Kati Clement-Frazier

INTRODUCTION

In the past 30 years, they have been repeatedly laid off, outsourced, replaced by information technology applications, and insulted with such derogatory names as "the cement layer." Their bosses accused them of distorting and disrupting communication in their organizations, and their subordinates accused them of thwarting the subordinates' autonomy and empowerment. Who are "they"? Middle managers—those managing in the middle of the organization.

With such treatment, you might think that middle managers are villainous evildoers who sabotage companies, or obstructionist bureaucrats who stand in the way of real work getting done. However, the reality is just the opposite. When performed well, the middle manager role is critical in organizations.

Although over the past several decades the value and stature of middle managers has seen both high and low points, we at Duke Corporate Education believe that managing in the center of the organization has always been both critically important and personally demanding. As one would expect, the essence of the role—the required mindset and skill set—has continued to change over time. The need to update each of these dimensions is driven by periodic shifts in such underlying forces as marketplace dynamics, technology, organizational structure, and employee expectations. Now and then, these forces converge to create a point of inflection that calls for a "step change" in how organizations are governed, with particular implications for those managing in the center.

In the *Leading from the Center* series, we examine some of these primary forces that are shaping what it means to successfully lead from the center in the modern organization. We outline the emerging imperative for middle management in an organization as well as the mindset, knowledge, and skills required to successfully navigate the most prevalent challenges that lie ahead.

THE NEW CENTER

Four powerful and pervasive trends affect the role that managers in the center of an organization are asked to assume. These trends—information technology, industry convergence, globalization, and regulations—connect directly to the challenges these managers face.

Compared to 20 or 30 years ago, *information technology* has escalated the amount, speed, and availability of data and changed the way we work and live. Access to information has shifted more power to our customers and suppliers. They not only have more information but are directly involved in and interacting with the various processes along the value chain. On a personal level, we now find ourselves connected to other people all the time; cell phones, pagers, BlackBerrys, and PDAs all reinforce the 24/7 culture. The transition from workweek to weekend and back is less distinct. Instead, microtransitions happen all day, every day, because many of us remain connected all the time.

Industries previously seen as separate are now seeing multiple points of *convergence*. Think about how digital technology has led to a convergence of sound, image, text, computing, and communications. Long-standing industry boundaries and parameters are gone (e.g., cable television companies are in the phone business, and electronics companies sell music) and along with them, the basis and nature of competition. When boundaries are blurred, new possibilities, opportunities, and directions exist, but it isn't always clear what managers should do. Managers will have to be prepared to adapt; their role is to observe, learn from experience, and set direction dynamically. Layered on top of this is the need to manage a more complex set of relationships—cooperating on Monday, competing on Tuesday, and partnering on Wednesday.

Globalization means that assets are distributed and configured around the world to serve customers and gain competitive advantage. Even companies that consider themselves local interact with global organizations. There is more reliance on fast-developing regional centers of expertise (e.g., computer programming in India and manufacturing in China). This means that middle managers are interacting with and coordinating the efforts of people who live in different cultures and may even be awake while their managers are asleep. The notion of a workday has changed as the work spans time zones. The nature of leading has changed as partnering with vendors and working in virtual teams across regions become more common.

The first three forces are causing shifts in the fourth—the *regulatory environment*. Many industries are experiencing more regulation, while a few others are experiencing less. Some arenas experiencing more regulation are also encountering a drive for more accountability. Demand for more accountability leads to a greater desire to clarify boundaries and roles. Yet both the rules and how best to operationalize them are more ambiguous than ever. Consider how, in the wake of Sarbanes-Oxley legislation, U.S. companies and their accountants continue to sort through the new requirements, while rail companies in Britain are negotiating which company is responsible for maintaining what stretch of tracks. Middle managers sit where regulations get implemented and are a critical force in shaping how companies respond to the shifts in the environment.

All of these changes have implications for those managing at the center of organizations. No small group at the top can have the entire picture, because the environment has more of everything: more information and connectivity, a faster pace, a dynamic competitive space, greater geographic reach, better informed and connected customers and suppliers, and shifting legal rules of the game. No small group can process the implications, make thoughtful decisions, and disseminate clear action steps. The top of the organization needs those in the center to help make sense of the dynamic environment. The connection between strategy development and strategy execution becomes less linear and more interdependent, and, therefore, managers in the center become pivotal actors.

As we said earlier, the notion of the middle of an organization typically conjures up a vertical image depicting managers in the center of a hierarchy. This mental image carries with it a perception of those managers as gatekeepers—controlling the pace at which information or resources flow down or up. It appears simple and linear.

However, as many of you are no doubt experiencing, you find yourselves navigating in a matrix and as a node in a network or multiple networks. As depicted in Figure I.1, this new view of the center conjures up images of centrality, integration, connection, and catalyst. *You are in the center of the action, not the middle of a hierarchy.*

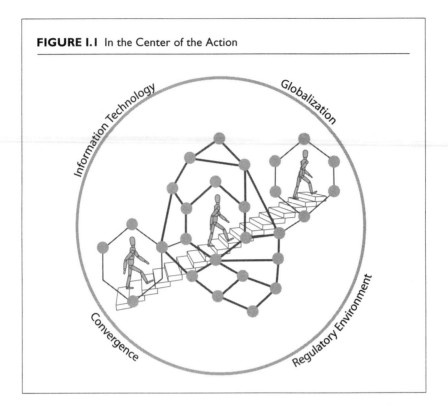

FIGURE I.1 In the Center of the Action

When you overlay this connected view on the traditional vertical notion, it produces some interesting tensions, trade-offs, and opportunities. Your formal authority runs vertically, but your real power to achieve results stems from your ability to work across all levels and boundaries.

IF YOU ARE LEADING FROM THE CENTER

If you are a manager in the center today, you have many hats to wear, more balls to juggle, and fewer certainties in your work environment. You have to be adaptive yet provide continuity in your leadership. You need to simultaneously translate strategy, influence and collaborate, lead teams, coach and motivate, support innovation, and own the systems and processes—all in the service of getting results. Those in the center need more courage than ever. You are the conscience of your organization, carrying forth its values, and at the same time you build today's and tomorrow's business success.

Strategy Translator

As a strategy translator, you must first understand the corporate strategy and determine what parts of it your group can best support. Next, you must translate it into an action plan for your group, making sure it aligns well to the overall strategy. You'll need to consider which projects are essential stepping stones and which are needed in their own right, and establish some priorities or guiding goals. You must then communicate the details of the plan and priorities and create momentum around them. As your team implements, you'll need to involve not only your people but also to collaborate and coordinate with others, including peers, customers, and other units. Instead of directing a one-way downward flow of information, you must translate upward as well and act as a conduit for strategic feedback to the executives above.

Influencer and Collaborator for Results

Middle managers must learn how to make things happen by influencing, integrating, and collaborating across the boundaries of the organization. As a manager, instead of focusing exclusively on your piece, you have to look outside of your own group to develop a network of supporting relationships. Rather than issuing commands and asserting power based on your position, you have to use other tactics to gain agreement and make things happen.

Leader of Teams

Teams have become a one-size-fits-all solution for organizing work in today's economy—virtual teams, project teams, product teams, and function-specific teams—and can be either the blessing or the bane of many companies. Your role as a manager includes understanding the challenges of teams and facilitating their development so that they can be effective more quickly. You have to align the team's energy and talents in a way that will deliver the desired results. You are responsible for creating an environment that will help this group of people work well together to achieve today's objectives and to develop the skills needed to take on future goals.

Coach and Motivator

Many organizations are well positioned to execute their strategies in yesterday's environment, are moderately able to meet their current needs, and often are not thinking at all about how to position themselves for the future. From the center of the organization, middle managers assume much of the responsibility for their people. They create an environment to attract and retain good employees, coach them to do their current jobs better, and bear primary responsibility for developing others. As a manager, you must figure out how to build the next level of capability, protect existing people, connect their aspirations to opportunities for development, and make work more enjoyable. You need to provide regular feedback—both positive and redirecting—and build strong relationships with those who surround you. If you do your job well, your departments will be more efficient, and your employees will be better equipped to become leaders in their own right.

Intrapreneur/Innovator

Enabling and supporting an innovative approach within your company will foster the strategic direction of the future. To effectively sponsor innovation, you need to create the context for your people, foster a climate that supports innovative efforts, and actively sponsor the ideas of the future. You have to *be* innovative and *lead* the innovative efforts of others. Innovation is most often associated with new-product development, but innovative approaches also are needed in developing new services or solving internal system and process problems. As a manager, you use your influence and relationships to find the root cause of problems and the resources to make change happen.

Owner of Systems and Processes

You need to understand that part of your role is to take ownership for designing and building new systems and processes. You will have to shift your thinking from living within existing systems and processes to making sure that those systems and processes work well: Do the systems and processes support progress or get in its way? One of the mistakes we have made in the past is not to hold managers accountable for their role in building the next generation of systems and processes. As a manager, you must perform harsh audits of existing systems and understand when to tear down what may have been left in place from a past strategy. You need to assess what is no longer relevant and/or is no longer working. Part of your responsibility is to evaluate and decide whether to reengineer or remove existing systems.

SHIFTS IN MINDSET NEEDED FOR THE FUTURE

In addition to the complex and shifting challenges that mid-level managers face in leading others, many are experiencing frequent changes in their own roles. The business environment is dynamic; and when new opportunities occur, companies must act quickly to take advantage of them. This may mean creating entire divisions, launching new offices in strategic locations, forming ad hoc project teams, or shifting strategic focus as a response. As a result, you may be asked to make a transition. It may be a new or vaguely defined role. It may be a lateral move. Or, you may "officially" stay in the same job, but the scope and scale of the work changes. Often, these kinds of changes happen with little guidance simply because the tasks are being defined in real time.

It's understandable that even the most experienced managers can find transitions challenging. Your ability to quickly adapt and become effective during a transition is critical to the organization's success; however, the need to move quickly doesn't change the fact that transitions take time, follow a predictable pattern, and contain some common traps. Transitions begin with a period of initial excitement at the challenge, where you may say yes to a change without really understanding what it means, fail to prepare others for the changes that are about to take place, and underestimate your own need to change. This is followed by a period of decreasing confidence and increasing doubt, when individuals may mistakenly try to hold on to a previous identity, or fail to connect with the right mix of people who can help them in their new identity. They reach a point where they consider whether and how they should continue in this transition, sometimes unable to see the options they have. Once they decide how to continue, they gradually work toward a level of increased confidence and transformation.

Transitions can also be much more difficult than anticipated as people work through what this means for their identity—how others see them, what skills and knowledge they will need, and how their beliefs and values align with the change in role.

In the following chapters we take a closer look at the transition process and the common traps that occur along the way. The goal isn't to avoid the process, but to understand it and accelerate how quickly and easily you become more comfortable and more effective in your new role.

CHAPTER ONE

THE CHALLENGE OF CHANGING ROLES

IN THIS CHAPTER

Role Changes and Transitions ■ The Transition Process ■ Changing
Identity May Be Harder ■ Looking Ahead

ROLE CHANGES AND TRANSITIONS

Throughout our lives, we take on different roles (e.g., student, employee, manager, novice, expert, coach, child, or parent). In our careers, we commonly expect to shift our focus, our responsibilities, and position over time. Change is inevitable; it's also often a desired and critical part of our progress and growth as leaders. Although people may want to take on new positions, changes in role start a period of transition for them, and for those around them, as they adapt and adjust.

Often, the change and ensuing transition is the result of a new job that you've not only agreed to but have been seeking—such as a promotion to a new position and level of responsibility within your organization. These types of role changes are often anticipated passages, ones for which you and your organization may have been preparing for and looking forward to. You may have attended training or received coaching or mentoring to prepare you for this change.

Perhaps you've been asked to make a lateral move into a new area with very different responsibilities. Maybe you've been tapped to lead a new team in an unfamiliar location. Perhaps you have been selected to lead an ad hoc or cross-functional project team where results are critical. Or, rather than experiencing a change in your role, you may find that the environment has changed around you. The business environment and the nature of work are dynamic. Even when your role "officially" stays the same, your job is often changing. The end result is that, even when you remain in your current position with the same title, office, and staff, your strategy, focus, and responsibilities can shift so dramatically that it *feels* as though you are in a new and unfamiliar role.

In short, you make a transition whenever you agree to a change in your current role. Whatever the situation, making transitions can land you in unfamiliar territory. Even the most experienced managers, those who have put considerable time and energy into developing their capabilities and professional identity, can find transitions challenging.

Not only do transitions come with challenges, but they come more often. Many find the frequency of their transitions has increased, more is at stake, and they need a different set of capabilities to succeed. We have less time to adapt—both because of frequent transitions and because others don't give us time. People are expected to transition quickly—to stretch into the assignment, get past the "unproductive" stage, and move on to getting results. The previous norm of getting slowly acclimated to a new role and gradually becoming more effective has become a luxury. Your ability to become effective quickly will be critical to the organization's success.

However, the need to move quickly does not change the fact that *transitions take time and follow a predictable pattern*. The goal isn't to skip the process altogether. In fact you shouldn't even try. Instead, the goal is to accelerate how quickly and with the least amount of pain you can navigate the transition process to become comfortable and effective in your new role.

Some aspects of your transition will typically be easier than others. You may adjust readily to visible changes—getting a new title, sitting in a new office, relocating, changing business cards, leading a different project team, interacting with new people, and joining new groups. However, other changes take more time, thought, and energy, such as:

- Acquiring new knowledge and skills
- Building a new network of relationships
- Rethinking your identity—how you view the world and yourself, and how you behave in light of that view

THE TRANSITION PROCESS

Although every situation and individual is unique, the passages that people navigate when they experience role changes and identity transitions follow a typical pattern. The transition process includes predictable zones in which people's sense of well-being and level of effectiveness will rise and fall. To varying degrees, one feels initial excitement, then uncertainty and doubt, inner unrest, and indecision about how to proceed, and finally, transformation to a new level of confidence and sense of identity.

Much of the early work studying life transitions focused on the psychological effects of negative events, such as family crisis, trauma, and bereavement, and the emotional stages that people go through as part of those transitions. Later research applied the same transition process to a number of major but positive life events—marriage, the birth of a child, promotion to a new job, moving to another country—which can cause just as much disruption and follow a similar transition process pattern. (Hopson, 1976)

We argue that a similar process is valid when applied to the changing roles and transitions that managers experience today. The transition process described below is adapted from Hopson's Transition Cycle. There is a common process, but people do not take a set path when going through a transition. As the image in Figure 1.1 conveys, people can vary in the degree to which they experience the highs and lows of excitement, uncertainty, doubt, choice, confidence, and transformation. Individuals will have different levels of highs and lows, depending on their particular situation. No two transitions feel identical.

FIGURE 1.1 The Transition Process

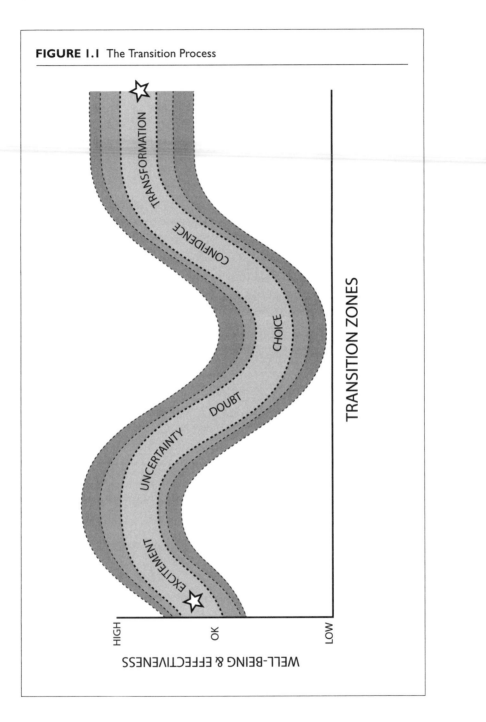

The Zone of Excitement

Nothing great was ever achieved without enthusiasm.
Ralph Waldo Emerson

Let's say an opportunity has presented itself that also signals a change in your current role and, to some degree, your professional identity. Whatever the opportunity—major promotion, leading a new project team, adding responsibilities to your existing role, or shifting laterally to another area of the company—it usually generates some degree of excitement at the prospect of something new. Reactions can range from a sense of elation if it's something you've been working toward, to eagerness to do well if it's unanticipated, to nervousness because it sounds like a real challenge. Your initial reaction may not be all positive; it might be a mix of emotions. Typically, though, when someone asks you to take on a new role, there is some pride or pleasure in being chosen. You have entered the zone of excitement.

Perhaps you are a first-time manager, eager to prove you are ready for this next step. Or maybe you're an experienced manager who has been promoted to a more senior leadership level. You may have decided to move into a new functional or geographic area where you have less expertise or to take lead responsibility for your first major client. Change events can vary widely in scope and visibility, yet each can represent a major transition.

At this stage, you may be thinking through the benefits of taking on the new position, envisioning what it will be like. You may just be smiling from ear to ear, enjoying the moment. Or maybe you have already jumped ahead and started making mental lists of what you will need to do to get ready.

This zone's activities form the foundation for your transition. What you do in this "honeymoon" phase will shape the speed and ease of your transition. Who do you tell first? What questions do you ask? How do you finish the work you have under way in your current position? How do you celebrate your new adventure?

The Zone of Uncertainty and Doubt

Our doubts are traitors, And make us lose the good we oft might win
By fearing to attempt.
William Shakespeare

The initial excitement of the honeymoon phase often starts to wane as you begin the day-to-day tasks—and you start to see that perhaps all isn't as you thought it would be. Much of your early attention was focused on whether you would *like* your new responsibilities, tasks, and so on. As you enter the zone of doubt, the focus then turns to whether you will actually be *good* at them. (Hill, 2003)

At this stage, you take a closer look at the skills and knowledge that you have versus what is required for this job. You may begin to suspect that someone made a mistake, that this role doesn't match who you are and what you can do. The reality may not align with the picture you had in your head. You realize that this role requires developing new relationships, new capabilities, and a new definition of self. You may find some changes and demands that you didn't anticipate:

- The stakes are higher or have a different focus.
- The players are different and perhaps more powerful.
- Your skills don't fit all that you need to do.
- You have additional or altered responsibilities.
- Your support system is not as effective.
- You don't have as much relevant experience to draw on.

Internally, you begin to experience increasing uncertainty and doubt: whether this is the job you signed up for, if it's a job you really want, what you should be doing, and how you should do it. Uncertainty creeps in about whether you are the right fit for this role: Do you have the capabilities you'll need to be successful? You may start to get wisps of negative thought sneaking in, questioning whether you should stay in this role at all.

With any change in role, it takes time to get the lay of the land and to grow into it. At the start, you might experience some ups and downs or an outcome or two that you view as failures. At this point, you have a good sense of how hard the task is. You may develop a sense of dread, unsure what to do. Left unchecked, uncertainty and doubt may continue to build, leading to even less confidence and more confusion. This point in the transition process truly is a slippery slope, and the zone of doubt and uncertainly may well plummet into a zone of terror.

Seeking and getting support at this point in the transition process is critical. In truth, no one goes through a transition alone. If you haven't already, you need to get others actively engaged.

The Zone of Choice

When written in Chinese, the word crisis is composed of two characters–one represents danger, and the other represents opportunity.
John Fitzgerald Kennedy

Your new role isn't going the way you expected or envisioned. Your doubts may have increased about your decision to accept this challenge or your ability to manage it successfully. Whether or not others think it's going okay, you may feel as though you're not doing enough soon enough. Or maybe you've gotten signals from others that you're not on a winning path. You feel as if failure is approaching, or you think it's already arrived. You don't know specifically what to do, but you realize that it's time to make some choices, select a path, and pursue it with energy and passion.

Returning to your previous role can feel terribly appealing–you were good at it. Sometimes this option is viable, although it often doesn't work as well as you might think. However, if the new role is not a good fit for you or for the company's needs, then exit is an option.

Or, instead of exiting, you can choose to change yourself and figure out what will make this new situation work–find more support, influence those around you, change parts of your own behavior or expectations. Despite lingering uncertainty and doubt, action and experimentation can help you discover a path to being more effective.

The Zone of Confidence and Transformation

It's no use going back to yesterday–because I was a different person then.
Lewis Carroll

You make some choices and decisions to move past your unease, uncertainty, and lack of confidence. You begin to take definite steps. You remind yourself that transformation won't happen overnight. It took awhile to get to this point, and it will take some time to move forward. Even as you begin working toward a successful transformation, you will still feel uncertainty. Although you may be confident about where you need to go, you may have doubts about the right way to proceed. Your path still depends on the relationships and support of others. Break it into smaller pieces, take one step at a time, and understand that the path may continue to have ups and downs as you go forward.

Just as the downward spiral of uncertainty and doubt can be a vicious cycle, the upward spiral of increasing confidence can be a virtuous one. Focus on securing some small wins, and use those to build your own confidence as well as others' confidence in you. As you make progress, people will be more willing to accept you in this different role and engage in working with you to achieve results.

CHANGING IDENTITY MAY BE HARDER

Moving your desk is relatively easy. Changing how you view yourself in a new role is much harder; sometimes it is the hardest part of making a transition successfully. As you work through the stages of the transition, you need simultaneously to tend to your identity shift. On several levels, this change in outside role will require you to make internal changes, including how you orient yourself toward others and the rest of the world. As with the transition process, this identity shift happens over time. Your identity has been constructed layer by layer over an extended period, and little of it is easily changed.

How do we describe ourselves? How do we express our identity? When you meet people for the first time, their view of your identity often begins with what you tell them. Most of us begin with our name, then add appropriate basic information that puts us in context for the other person. For example, in a meeting with new project members, you might identify yourself by your department, title, how long you've been with the company, or what role you'll be playing in that group. In social situations, you might share where your house is in relation to a neighbor's, which kid on the soccer field is yours, or how you're acquainted with the bride or groom.

Even when you don't specifically provide information, people make deductions about your identity through visible symbols—a white coat and stethoscope, a hard hat, a guitar case, a wedding ring, a uniform, a nametag, or press pass. These outer accessories may symbolize a certain level of training, experience, or status to others. If you wear a pilot's uniform and enter a plane's cockpit, passengers will infer that you have been tested and certified in your ability to fly this particular plane. Your identity, however, is more complex than just what these symbols indicate.

As Figure 1.2 details, your identity has several layers. Some outer layers are easily adapted, while others are deeply held and immutable. Changes may occur from the outside in or from the inside out. Depending on the particular transition you are experiencing, you may notice only a change in outer layers of your identity, such as developing a new skill or creating a new routine. In other cases, you may need to make some fundamental shifts in how you think about yourself and how you interact with others as you grow and change as an individual. Although the process may at first be unexpected and disorienting, this level of identity discovery and reinvention can be the most rewarding.

The Inner Layers

At the center of our identity is a core that we'll call the "DNA layer." It defines who we are at the most basic level. That center is unique and present from an early age; it is the personality traits and preferences that we have shown for as long as we can remember. These talents just seem to be there, letting you accomplish tasks that others have to work hard to master.

- *Personality and preferences* help define the way that you prefer to work, interact with others, and make choices when given options. Personality profiles such as the Myers-Briggs Type Indicator are designed to help us recognize our preferences and how they affect the way that we think, act, and interact with

FIGURE 1.2 Layers of Identity

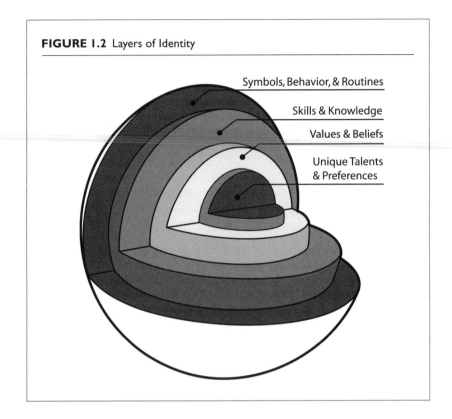

Symbols, Behavior, & Routines

Skills & Knowledge

Values & Beliefs

Unique Talents & Preferences

others. Preferences aren't defined as good or bad, or right or wrong, but simply as present, such as how you make decisions or process information.

- *Talents* are your unique and natural abilities, aptitudes, or ways of thinking that you instinctively draw on to navigate and work through your daily experiences. These might include analytical, artistic, or physical talents; perhaps you're naturally good at crunching numbers or designing the flow of presentations. When you use your talents, tasks seem easier and more enjoyable.

Another part of your inner identity is a layer of values and beliefs that have developed over time. They help define how you perceive yourself and your actions relative to others or an outside standard. These are deeply embedded and color how you interpret the environment around you.

- *Values* are your moral compass. They define the behaviors you think are desirable, should be respected, and should guide how you and others interact in the world. Values develop largely out of your direct experiences with people who are important to you—parents, friends, and mentors—and are based on how they behave toward you and others. Your values define what behaviors you think are right or wrong, good or bad, desirable or undesirable, and ethical or unethical. They guide your daily interactions in many ways and your judgments and understandings about your own and others' identities.

- *Beliefs* are the concepts that you consider to be true and self-evident. They define your theory of how the world works, or at least how it should work. Your nationality, background, culture, and directly relevant experiences in life and at work all influence your beliefs. You naturally develop beliefs about your industry, your business, what it means to be a leader, and how to interact with others. For example, as a manager, you likely have formed beliefs about how to inspire others.

As you take on new roles, challenges, and situations, you may feel moved to rethink beliefs and values that you hold dear or to consider some for the first time. For example, many people relate that becoming a parent not only adds a new facet to their identity but also triggers a process of self-discovery. This may be the first time that they have to evaluate their own values and beliefs in terms of the type of parent they want to be—setting appropriate limits and discipline, creating a home environment, selecting an approach to education, or being a role model. This shift typically occurs from the outside in; others first recognize you as a parent, and then you acquire some skills and knowledge for the role (feeding, diapering, etc.). And gradually your inner identity shifts to accommodate what the role really means.

The Outer Layers

Your capabilities are developed over time and are more often in a state of change. As you progress through a combination of formal education and on-the-job experience, your skills and knowledge are extended—at times more broadly and at times more deeply. You may not recognize each situation as a learning opportunity at the moment that it occurs, especially if the task was one that you struggled with. However, all such tasks help to build your future capabilities.

- *Skills* are about knowing how to do something and can be taught. They can also span a range of categories, effort to develop, and levels of expertise. For example, knowing how to access the latest sales data may be one skill level, whereas generating reports on client reorders may be another. You typically have several options to obtain help and support from others, such as attending training classes, shadowing others, asking questions, or seeking coaching.
- *Knowledge* is gained through the information, understanding, and connections that you build through both experience and study. For example, through your interactions with a particular client company, you might learn more about their key issues and strategic direction, gaining knowledge that will serve you well in your interactions with them.

The outermost layer of identity is the most visible and the most easily adapted and changed. This layer defines who you are in relation to other people (a manager, a daughter, a coach, or service provider), whether you have authority to act and make decisions, and what resources you control.

- *Symbols* are those signs that others can easily observe and use to understand your identity. They vary and are often a by-product of the culture and environment of the organization. Some are direct symbols, such as a new office or placement on the organizational chart. Other indicators may be more indirect, such as an invitation to sit at the table during executive sessions, the size or location of your office, or a choice parking space.

- *Behaviors* are used by others to observe and evaluate you in a new role. Do they see you modeling the behaviors of a good manager? Have you demonstrated that you are a credible advisor or a trustworthy and high-quality service provider? All of these and more affect how others see you and how you see yourself reflected back.

- *Routines* are the physical and visible rhythms within which you work. They can be a way to reinforce your identity and the messages that you deliver verbally. They can be checking in for 20 minutes with your boss once a week, having lunch once a month with peers, making a point to welcome all new employees personally during their first week at work, or starting each morning by reviewing and adjusting your schedule and to-do list.

Transitioning to a new or different role can require peeling away some of these layers and rethinking or reconstructing your identity. This complex process can at times feel threatening. For example, if you pride yourself on being a great technician but are no longer doing technical work, you may feel as if you have lost a piece of your professional identity and are not as valuable or useful. Part of the transition process will be finding the right pieces to reconstruct the sense of self that is now missing.

Remember, transitions will come in all different shapes and sizes. Some will go as you anticipated, and others will hold surprises. They will almost certainly trigger some degree of change for you, but that, too, will vary. Transitions will almost always require some degree of change to the outer layers of your identity. Some may require that you change locations and interact with a new group of people; others may require that you work hard at developing a new skill that you are lacking. Not every transition will prompt you to rethink your point of view as to how the world can and should work and how you need to interact with it—but some do.

LOOKING AHEAD

Over the next eight chapters, we will take the trip through the transition process and the actions people can take to make it a smoother and faster journey. Although we can't insulate you from either the changes or the identity threat, we do hope to make them both easier. In Chapter 2, we lay out the common traps people encounter as they transition. In the remaining chapters, we explore each trap in more detail: what it is and how it happens, what the results of falling into it can be, and how to avoid it.

CHAPTER TWO

THE TRANSITION TRAPS

IN THIS CHAPTER

Transition Implications for Today's Manager ■ Guiding Ideas
■ The Journey Is Filled with Traps ■ Personal Reflections

TRANSITION IMPLICATIONS FOR TODAY'S MANAGER

Companies have typically recognized the need for learning and support during major role transitions, and they have focused their attention on the big steps—becoming a first-time manager, moving to the director level, or advancing to the executive suite. The assumption was that managers would remain within a single company, occasionally making a major transition to a new level. Once there, they would spend some time becoming more comfortable and competent in that role before being ready for another transition.

The reality is quite different. The nature of work today is that changes in roles or responsibilities are commonplace, happening so fast and frequently that some people may feel as if they are always in transition. People don't stay in the same job as long as they did in the past; instead, movement is rapid both for those who stay with the company and for those who depart for other organizations. New marketplace opportunities emerge, and companies must work quickly to take advantage of them. Top management creates new divisions, launches offices in strategic locations, and forms new ad hoc project teams in response. People may find themselves simultaneously navigating multiple transitions.

Transitions are also more frequent because the nature of the employment contract is changing. Today's workers don't want to change roles nonstop, but neither do they expect (nor want, perhaps) to work for decades within the same area or division, or even for the same company. They see greater opportunities for growth and learning by expanding their experience beyond their current role, beyond a few employers, or even beyond industries. (Johnson, 2005)

The U.S. Bureau of Labor Statistics (BLS) is frequently asked for data on how many jobs the average person holds in a lifetime—a number that would require tracking the same respondents over their entire working lives. So far, no survey has ever tracked respondents for that long. However, a survey begun in 1979 has tracked younger baby boomers over a large portion of their lives.

A BLS report published in August 2002 examined the number of jobs that people born in the years 1957 to 1964 held from age 18 to age 36. These younger baby boomers held an average of 9.6 jobs from ages 18 to 36. In this report, a job is defined as an uninterrupted period of work with a particular employer. (Bureau of Labor Statistics, 2002)

Attempting to estimate the number of times people make career shifts in the course of their working lives is nearly impossible. One of the difficulties is that no real consensus exists on what constitutes a career change. For example, if a construction worker decides to start a home-remodeling business, is that a career change? What about a mechanical engineer who quits to teach physics and math in a high school?

Perhaps you can now see the difficulty in estimating the frequency with which people are experiencing transitions—small or large—in their roles. Although there are no hard statistics, our experience with clients tells us that change continues to increase and that people need help in managing this trend.

Managers are making a multitude of lower-profile transitions as they lead cross-functional projects, add new departments to their areas, and expand their responsibility, often beginning another transition while still in the midst of a previous one. As transitions have become more prevalent, the guidance available to help managers through the process has not kept up, so confusion and uncertainty are understandable outcomes. Sometimes the complexity arises because it's difficult to define what you are transitioning to. People are frequently put in new circumstances where their charge is vague and the rules of the game are evolving as they go. It's difficult to understand and define the new role, because it is being defined in real time; there are no models to follow or mentors to lead the way.

Once you have said yes to your new job or task, your initial excitement and the thrill of the challenge may be short-lived if you feel pressure to produce results but aren't sure how. You need to meet others' expectations while you work through changes to your identity, relationships, and tasks. After a time, you may begin to recognize some key points that you missed initially—what the new role actually entails, how complex or vague the tasks are, or what capabilities you lack. You may lose confidence and perhaps develop a mild sense of panic. After some time, you come to learn that you will have to make some choices about what to do differently, because you can't continue on the current path and be successful. Your choices may require developing new relationships, new capabilities, or a new definition of self as you work toward becoming more effective.

Many of the transition difficulties that people experience are clear, and once you know what they are, you can avoid them. The tips and tools that we offer in this book won't allow you to skip steps, but they can help you reduce the time you spend in the zone of uncertainty and doubt, instead moving quickly to become effective in this new space.

GUIDING IDEAS

If we know that transitions share a common pattern, what can you do to make them easier for yourself and others? How can you maintain your balance during the predictable periods of doubt and uncertainty and avoid the treacherous downhill slide where doubt turns into terror? How can you transition and transform your identity with the least amount of pain for yourself or others? One way is to keep the following guiding ideas in mind:

- *Awareness can smooth the way and lessen the pain.* People experience a typical pattern during a transition concerning how they feel about themselves, the steps they go through, and their effectiveness. There are also some common points along the way that cause difficulties. Being aware of the pattern and common traps can help you prepare better for transitions when they occur, smoothing the way through some of these traps or avoiding them altogether. The faster you can navigate the transition traps, the more quickly you will become effective and comfortable in your new role. So recognize when you are in transition, and use this awareness to help you work through it.
- *Don't expect an overnight transformation.* People can't change instantly. Awareness may help to accelerate and smooth the way, but it can't eliminate the process. It takes time, and as much as you'd like to, you can't skip any steps. It's important to have realistic expectations about what can and will change quickly and what will occur more slowly. This awareness is a challenge, because often people set expectations based on external cues, such as title or office location, and don't realize that the individual can't yet meet those new expectations.

  People need to be aware of and prepare for the entire spectrum of behavioral changes. Some outward changes can happen quickly (different titles, offices, locations, parking spaces, or routines for meetings and calls) and are easily visible. Other changes will occur over time. For example, you may not feel completely capable right away; however, your skills and knowledge will develop, as will your experience and confidence in your capabilities. As you demonstrate greater competence to yourself and others, shifts may also occur in decision making, culture, and relationships. It's important to view change and your experiences in context and adapt your expectations accordingly.

- *Realize that no one goes through it alone.* You can create the greatest leverage by being proactive and making choices. Take charge of your own learning and development by reaching out to engage others early in the process. Don't assume that you have to work your way through a transition alone, and don't wait until you are struggling, uncertain, or depressed to reach out. Saving face may help your pride; however, never reaching out means no help and makes the transition process more difficult and lengthy.

  Be sure to negotiate and renegotiate your relationships during the entire transition process. Be aware of those around you—how they're reacting to the change and how they can help you with this transition.

- *Invest in yourself—it's worth it.* Take time to consider what would be most helpful to you during this transition, and invest time and energy in getting the things you need. Recent college graduates often joke that, even if they don't know what they're doing, just showing up for the first day of work in a new suit goes a long way in boosting their confidence and self-image. For you, it may mean taking a class to get a better grounding in financial basics. It may mean seeking a coach or mentor to guide and support you as you learn and practice new skills. It may mean routinely setting aside some time at the end of each day to be reflective and plan next steps or taking a long weekend to recharge. Even small things, like a daily planner and stylish pen, if they help, are worthwhile investments. It's also worthwhile to better understand the nature of the transition process and how to navigate through the passage. So consider time spent reading this book as an investment in you.

THE JOURNEY IS FILLED WITH TRAPS

Another step in successfully navigating your way through a transition is to *be aware of the common traps that occur in each of the transition zones and prepare better for them.*

As you can see in Figure 2.1, several traps can interfere with your progress when you are just starting out and still in the zone of Excitement:

- Not understanding what you're saying yes to
- Failing to prepare others for the change
- Underestimating your own need to change

Although it may be easy to ignore or miss these traps, because you're focusing on the potentially positive aspects of the opportunity, these traps are real and can derail you. It is your ability to avoid this combination of early traps that will determine how quickly and easily you can make your way past the zones of Uncertainty and Choice to a successful Transformation. If you fall into too many of these traps, you will have a hard time getting others' support and commitment.

As your initial excitement begins to wane and the need for real change and transition becomes more evident, you enter the zone of Uncertainty and Doubt where some additional traps await:

- Mistakenly hanging onto your previous identity
- Not getting the right mix of people on board to help you

In both cases, you haven't adapted enough soon enough to ensure smooth sailing.

The degree to which you experience uncertainty and doubt and thus find yourself in the zone of Choice will depend largely on how well you have navigated the previous traps, as each can in some way ease or compound the complexity of the next. If you navigate them well, you should have support as you change and assume your new role. If you don't, you can wind up feeling alone. Falling prey to several of the previous traps can increase the level of transition crisis you experience—and create the next trap:

- Thinking that you don't have any choice

As we'll see when we take a closer look at this zone, you actually have multiple options.

FIGURE 2.1 The Transition Process Traps

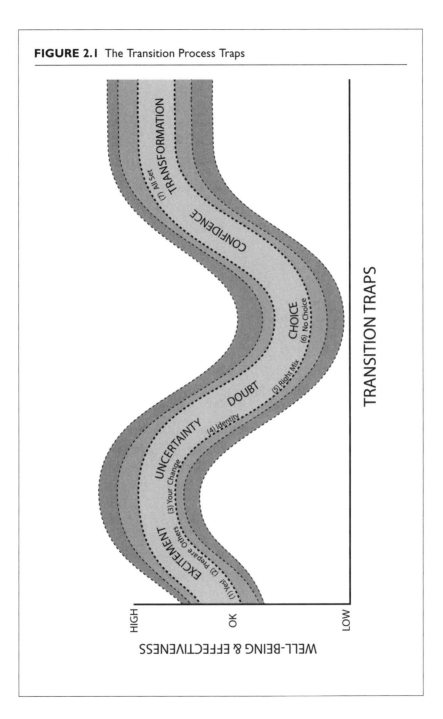

As you make a decision and plan for moving past the zone of Choice, you will likely begin to feel more confident as you experiment with different approaches and experience some success. The zone of Confidence and Transformation can feel a little like the initial zone of excitement you experience at the outset—you are relieved to have made a decision, to be moving forward and making progress. Don't fall into the final trap, however:

- Thinking that your transition is "finished" and you are all set

Even if you feel you've made the right choice, this final zone can be a little rocky as you go through the process of trial and error in figuring out how to implement it.

Within this book, we take a closer look at each of the transition zones and the traps that lie within, and we learn more about how to recognize them, how others have experienced them, and how to successfully work through them. Each chapter invites an opportunity to reflect on transitions that you may have experienced in the past or may even be experiencing now. Forewarned is forearmed; understanding the traps will help with your current or your next transition.

PERSONAL REFLECTIONS

As we've noted, changes to your role and the associated degree of transition will vary in frequency and scope. We encourage you to take a moment to reflect on the variety of transitions you have already experienced, or are perhaps experiencing now, before reading more about the traps that you can avoid:

- Did you recognize that the change would require a transition? How easily were you able to go through the process?
- To what degree did you experience each of the transition zones—Excitement, Uncertainty and Doubt, Choice, and Confidence and Transformation? Which presented the most difficulty?
- Which traps did you become victim to, and how did you get past them?

- As you experienced this transition, in what ways do you think your identity evolved (or is still evolving) in terms of
  - symbols, behaviors, and routines;
  - skills and knowledge; and
  - values and beliefs?

CHAPTER THREE

FIRE, AIM, READY!

IN THIS CHAPTER

What Did You Just Agree To? ■ Consequences of Saying Yes
Too Quickly ■ Caught Up in the Thrill ■ It's No Big Deal
■ What to Do

WHAT DID YOU JUST AGREE TO?

Whatever transition you find yourself in the midst of—major promotion, new project or team, shifting responsibilities—you can feel excitement at being "chosen." That initial excitement, anticipation, or thinking you already know what's in store can lead you to **say yes quickly, perhaps a bit too quickly, without really understanding** *what* **you're saying yes to.**

A change in role can be the culmination of hard work and concentrated effort. You may have been aspiring to this opportunity for quite some time. If so, you probably have some preconceived beliefs about what it will be like when you achieve it. In the zone of Excitement, we tend to focus on the positives, anticipating the possibilities of what's to come. You may see this as the opportunity you've been waiting for and feel eager to handle more responsibility, lead others, weigh in on critical decisions, or operate on a broader scale. The new role may be in a critical growth area in your company that moves you toward a senior leadership position. As such, you've spent a considerable amount of time thinking about the role and how you'd perform in it, maybe even romanticizing it a bit.

In another scenario, this opportunity may not be one that you've necessarily been seeking but one that is nevertheless critical to the company's future. So you want to step up to the challenge. It will almost certainly be difficult, but the role is vital and you have been selected for the job. Someone believes that you have what it takes to merge two divisions, to turn that lagging department around, or get that project back on track. Any combination of forces can take over—your sense of company loyalty, personal commitment to your boss, or perhaps your competitive spirit—and you readily sign up for the challenge, firing the starting gun to begin the process of your transition before you really know what kind of race you're in.

On the other hand, you may say yes too quickly because you underestimate the significance or scope of what you're being asked to do. The request doesn't sound that complex, and many other people were also capable of stepping up to the task, but they asked you, so you take it on. Rather than feeling a need to prove yourself capable of the task, you approach the change in responsibility and your own transformation with a feeling that this will be business as usual.

For any number of logical reasons, you may say, "Yes!" Although any transition offers potentially positive *and* negative aspects, we often tend to focus on the positive aspects and miss potential downsides. Such an oversight can create fertile ground for problems down the road. Even if you feel as if you can't say no, you should at least begin with a better-informed yes. That alone can be a big step toward successfully navigating the transition.

CONSEQUENCES OF SAYING YES TOO QUICKLY

If you don't anticipate some of the dimensions of your changing role—required skills, areas of focus, levels of commitment, shift in authority, daily interactions, others' expectations—you may have trouble. You might set off with the wrong assumptions about what you should be doing, what skills and knowledge you will need, or what effects these changes will have on your daily life. When you aren't clear or don't negotiate what yes really means, falling victim to this trap can produce any one of several negative effects.

You Begin Doing the Wrong Job

You might underestimate what the change in role will actually mean for your work on a day-to-day basis. You step in but don't really understand what you should be doing. For example, your company has decided that all project managers in each division will meet monthly to increase connections across groups, hopefully improving processes. The intent is that people will share best practices, common problems, and issues. You've been asked to lead those group meetings. You interpret the task as a two-hour per month commitment and a nice chance to get together with some former colleagues. In reality, it turns out to be an important effort at addressing some critical gaps in effectiveness. Only later do you discover that you not only need to facilitate the discussions but also to follow up on the issues people raise and take recommendations to your boss and the leaders of other divisions. Many of those leaders then seek one-on-one time with you to push their personal agendas. You start to realize that the two-hour meeting once a month is really eight hours every week. You thought you were saying yes to an easy addition, but it turned out quite differently.

Alternatively, when you overestimate the role, you can end up trying to do more than you should or can effectively do. When you aim your limited resources and energy in too many different directions, they can become diluted—having little impact or effect. Or you may agree to take on too much and risk burning out. For instance, people know you're a great coach and mentor, so your boss asks you to help others become better at mentoring. The boss pictures you leading a single, brown-bag lunch talk; you take the assignment as creating a companywide mentoring program with workshops, lunches, and logo-festooned giveaways.

In either case, you end up doing the wrong job. Not getting the requirements, responsibilities, and expectations as close to right as you can before you agree to the role can have continued effects downstream on your ability to successfully navigate the transition.

You Fail to Develop the Capabilities You Need

If you don't clearly understand the scope of what you're being asked to take on, you can't accurately assess how well-suited you are for the role. We don't mean that you should have all of the capabilities that you need immediately. However, you do need to accurately assess what capabilities you will need and decide how to build the ones you don't yet have. Having an inaccurate picture of where you stand can lead you to make uninformed decisions about how easy or difficult this task will be, then waste valuable time once you decide to move forward.

For example, Nigel, a salesperson at a large, European industrial materials company, was promoted to sales manager, a position to which he had aspired. He was now in charge of five associates, monitoring their field calls and sales. It sounded right up his alley—after all, Nigel knew the ins and outs of sales calls well, having spent five years in the position he was now supervising. However, he had given no thought to his management style (he had none) or the new routines or skills he would need. Over the first few months, he struggled with the transition from colleague to manager. He thought he'd just have to track the numbers, give pep talks to the associates, hold regular meetings, and so on. In reality, Nigel's beliefs about what a manager does were off target. As his confidence dipped, Nigel worried that his associates were abusing his lack of experience—trying to be buddies with him to divert his attention from their lower sales figures, giving barely plausible excuses for lack of activity, and generally running over him. Realizing this was not a good fit and that he was not prepared for the role of manager, Nigel finally brought the situation to his boss (before his boss could bring it up with him!) and decided to transition to a nonmanagerial position. It was a hard lesson to learn, but Nigel now knows that he needs to be better prepared before taking on a greater role.

So asking questions up front will let you gauge how well you currently match the proposed role and whether the skills you'll need to develop are ones that interest you. Otherwise, you may find yourself having to give speeches to large groups when your introverted nature cries out for one-on-one discussions.

You Aren't Prepared for the Changes

Depending on the scope of your transition, not only your life may change. In the Excitement phase, it is easy to romanticize all of the good things that will happen and forget to consider how the lives of those connected to you may also be affected. This includes, but isn't limited to, your close family members. Look across your entire network of relationships—family, friends, colleagues. How will your new role affect the connections that you have with close friends, organizations you belong to, groups that you volunteer for, associates or peers who you coach or mentor, or clients who see you as their primary contact? You might say yes without understanding that the new role means a heavy travel schedule, odd hours, or having to move to another city for a time.

Dig deeper and ask hard questions of yourself and others. What is this role change, and what does it mean for you and those around you?

CAUGHT UP IN THE THRILL

Geoff began his career in the advertising business. During his 17 years in the field, he progressed through the ranks to become one of the top five people in his organization. He was creating a very comfortable life for himself and his family, but after a few years, he began to feel as though he was too young to feel *this* comfortable in his job. Even though his family was wholly dependent on his income and he was very good at what he was doing, he was anxious to take on new and different career challenges.

That opportunity came during the dot.com boom of the 1990s, when a former client with $25 million in funding contacted him about providing the advertising for a technology start-up initiative. Geoff won the business and, during the course of his work, the CEO of the start-up asked Geoff to come work for them. The thrill of being chosen and of a possible overnight fortune made the job an exciting and challenging opportunity. Geoff would have to move his family somewhere unfamiliar and put his kids in new schools. However, given his desire for new challenges and the potential financial boon the position offered, he quickly accepted the job.

Leaving his family behind, Geoff spent six months commuting to Washington, D.C., helping the company get started. He felt as though he was reasonably equipped to handle this transition and that his marketing experience would parlay easily to a client-side position. What he didn't anticipate was that outside the advertising world, marketing is not always seen as a powerful business tool. He left an environment where his functional marketing expertise drove everything and went to a business where marketing was viewed as a "necessary evil." He wasn't able to develop arguments powerful enough to convince his senior management why they needed to invest in marketing. His difficulties were magnified in light of reduced capital funding and a softening economy—the dot.com bubble was bursting.

While still in the process of relocating his family, Geoff realized that he had accepted a position for which he was not well equipped, and at a company that didn't share his point of view. He had gotten caught up in the external vision of this new identity—the potential of being a high-tech millionaire, the thrill of being sought out by the CEO, and the excitement of something new—and didn't fully internalize the underlying requirements of the role. His knowledge and skills gaps were large, but more importantly, his values and beliefs about the role and value of marketing and how to get work done weren't consistent with what was needed. Six months later, he was out of a job. He hadn't even unpacked the moving boxes when he lost the job.

Losing his job put Geoff and his family in a very challenging position for a couple of years. The economy was declining, and he was in an entirely new market where he didn't know many people. During that time he learned a lot about the power of networks, the power of leveraging expertise, and the consequences of saying yes too quickly. He also learned about determination, courage, and the value of supportive family and friends. After a thoughtful search, Geoff has a very successful career now in a job he loves.

IT'S NO BIG DEAL

Gisele was excited as she took on a new task: coordinating an outside law firm and in-house counsel to produce a report for the Ontario government. This was the first time her company needed to submit the report, so hiring external lawyers who had been compiling such reports for years made sense. Relying on outsiders for significant legal work was uncharted territory, but it seemed an easy way to get the work done quickly and correctly and for the internal team to learn how to produce future reports. She'd personally verified that the external firm had done this type of work before and recommended them for this work. What's to worry?

Brimming with confidence in the outsiders, Gisele was certain that, for a large part of this project work, she would be able to take a back seat and monitor the process. Perhaps she would provide guidance when needed, but largely she planned to stay in the background as the real experts got busy. She coordinated meetings for the other firm to gather the raw data, provided some high-level direction at the outset, and then confidently stepped out of the way to let the ship sail forth.

Gisele's beliefs about how to inspire people and how others should be working didn't align well with this new task, and the ship ran aground pretty quickly. What had seemed to be a relatively straightforward question of organizing information and capable resources suddenly became a much more demanding situation. The outsiders had different expectations about how much Gisele and her team would do—they expected more than she could give them. In addition, their views of what "draft ready" meant were out of sync; the early drafts were nothing like what her firm had expected.

Gisele found herself swimming in an unpredicted sea of responsibilities: keeping her top management happy, editing draft reports, contributing to the data analysis, and even creating sections of the final report. Not only that, her boss and top management were watching closely as this first experiment in outsourcing unfolded; she felt she had to perform—and perform well. Getting the report out in a way that met all the legal requirements demanded triple the time that she had anticipated, leading to late nights and weekends and an increasing sense of desperation.

In the end, Gisele stepped back from the situation and called a few key meetings with the outside lawyers, where she outlined again what they had promised to deliver. After several tense discussions, the external firm switched its team, assigning more senior and experienced people to the project. What started out as "no big deal" rapidly exploded before Gisele ultimately managed to shepherd it home.

WHAT TO DO

Simply put, stop making assumptions and start asking the hard questions. Don't be deterred if the answers are incomplete. The complex nature of today's business world may mean that it's just not possible to get definitive answers to all of your questions. Often, people aren't withholding information; they simply don't have the answer, given the dynamic environment in which we work. Be prepared for uncertainty and ambiguity in some of the answers you receive, but don't let that stop you from asking the questions. Get as much detail as you can up front, and even after you have made the decision to say yes, continue to ask questions as you go and learn as much as you can before you are on the job.

Learn More about What You Would Need to Do

- *What does the job, task, or project really entail?* Describe to your boss what you think the role is and see if you are on track. Does it match your manager's view?
- *How far will the change in your responsibilities extend beyond the physical office?* Will more time be required outside normal work hours? It may include travel or more evening social commitments.
- *How well does the role align with what you want to do?* Ask yourself if this role is central to your career aspirations; it should help you build skills or gain experience for your next step. Consider also what types of activities you would spend the most time doing—such as time in the field with clients, coaching direct re-

ports, coordinating with peers, or reviewing statistical data and writing reports.

- *How does this opportunity connect to the larger organizational strategy?* Is it central to the company? Consider if this role will create more options for you in the future.
- *How would others describe this role?* Who is in the best position to give you good information? Seek multiple viewpoints, both internally and externally. Some good sources may be others who currently have similar positions within the company. Additional sources are those who can give insight (clients, vendors, other teams) into the current status of a particular project or team who will be part of your responsibility.
- *Focus on both potential positives* and *negatives.* Think about what you know about the proposed role. Consider what you don't know yet. In every job, people love some parts, while they do other parts because they're required. Do you know approximately the proportion of tasks you like to tasks you are required to perform? You might also ask yourself or others how they would see this opportunity: Why would others be reluctant to pursue this opportunity? or Why would others enthusiastically pursue it?

Learn More about What Capabilities You Will Need

- *Ask yourself why you are being offered the opportunity for this role change.* Honestly assess how you view your own capabilities as they relate to this opportunity. How big a stretch is it from what you are doing today? Do you think you are ready for this change? Why or why not?
- *Ask others why they think you were offered this opportunity.* "Why does the company think I am well suited for this? What strengths do they think I have that will work well? What challenges do you think I need to actively work on?" As much as you are able, ask those who have some insight into both your capabilities and this role to provide some feedback.

- *What skills, knowledge, and competencies will be critical right away?* Which can be developed over time? Consider if this role will provide you an opportunity to build new skills.
- *If gaps exist between your current capabilities and what you would need in the future, identify the gaps and plan how to build the skills and knowledge that you need.* Some organizations have internal resources available, such as coaching or training. In some cases, you may need to look for external resources to bridge the gap, such as management seminars, professional coaching, or development programs.
- *How will your performance be evaluated?* You should try to get a clear picture of what success would look like. Consider how long a grace period you will have before you will have to produce results. Try to align your expectations with those of your boss, particularly around how long you will have to adjust to the new role and what your ultimate responsibilities will be.

Learn More about How You and Others Will Need to Adapt

- *How and where will you need support?* Have you asked others for their support?
- *Will you have less or more time for nonwork activities, large and small?* Think about vacations, weekend getaways, evenings out, kids' events, hobbies, or volunteering.
- *Which of your personal commitments will need to shift to others?* You can only do so much. Think about your family obligations and who will meet them: providing transportation, minding budgets, doing shopping, making or keeping appointments, etc. Given your new role, will your external commitments need to change, even for a short period of time? Consider the time commitments you have with volunteering, recreation, or hobbies.
- *Which of your current work responsibilities are better delegated to others?* Ask yourself if your direct reports can take on tasks such as presentations, planning, client meetings, or travel. Sometimes obligations to peers and other colleagues have to change: Which committees or project teams, planning, or client re-

sponsibilities will you continue to do versus having someone else step in?

- *What are others' expectations?* You are not the only one affected by this change. Other people will have to decide what they will take on to help you or what they will give up.

So before saying yes, be sure to ask questions and understand what you're saying yes to. It helps to go in with a realistic view of the new position. You should also consider how your saying yes will affect others. In the next chapter, we explore our second trap: not preparing those around you for your change.

CHAPTER FOUR

FORE!

IN THIS CHAPTER

Preparing Others ■ Recognizing the Ripple Effects
■ Expanding Your Identity ■ What to Do

PREPARING OTHERS

Fore is another word for *ahead* (think of a ship's fore and aft). Calling "Fore!" is also a quick and simple way for golfers to yell "Watch out ahead!", alerting others that an errant ball is on its way and giving them some time to prepare—a warning that most people appreciate. Just as you need time to prepare for a change, so do those around you. However, in the initial excitement or anticipation, managers may forget to warn others. A common transition trap is **forgetting to prepare those around you for the changes that are about to take place.**

When your role changes within an organization, you don't just have a new office and title or more staff and tasks. In many ways, the social fabric may loosen or come undone—both for you and for those with whom you have been interacting. Don't assume that you alone will experience the effects of this transition. As your role shifts, your working relationships will shift as well. The more obvious primary relationships with your direct reports and boss can be affected, but so can secondary relationships with those you (or others) look to for coaching and advice, consider peers, or hold accountable for results.

Not only may your work relationships be affected by your change in role. Personal relationships are likely to feel the effects of change as well, and those people may also need to be prepared. Be assured that you will need their support.

Although taking on this new challenge may be exciting for you, others may not share your enthusiasm. You may have anticipated the change and its implications, having thought about this opportunity and worked toward it. Or maybe you hadn't expected it, but you have at least had time to consider it, ask questions, and get comfortable with the notion. Others, however, may receive your news and quickly have to adapt. For them, the transition may feel sudden, and they may feel as if they had no say in the matter.

Your transition doesn't have to feel like a bolt of lightning from a clear sky for others, but if it does, it easily can have a negative effect both on your relationships and your ability to successfully work through the transition. Remember, your future success depends in part on others' support and assistance.

Recall the transition process image from Chapter 1. Your new opportunity may trigger phases of excitement, uncertainty, doubt, choice, and transformation for others as well. Just as you are navigating your way through these changes and what they mean for your relationships and identity, others will be navigating their own path at their own speed. You and they may very well have different starting points (their initial enthusiasm may not match your own), and along the way, your feelings of well-being and effectiveness may be out of sync as you experience the transition in different ways. You may be going along feeling pretty good about how things are going, while others are becoming frustrated by the effects the change is having on them. The opposite may also be true, if your doubt is building while they assume everything is fine.

In many cases, if those around you aren't prepared, they can't work through their own reactions to the change. Some may feel hurt that they were "left out" of your decision making and not consulted on something so important. They may have been left out because you thought the changes would be minimal and didn't anticipate that others would be affected. Or they may have been left out because you simply weren't able to discuss it with anyone. The change may have happened too quickly to allow time to touch base with as many people as you would have liked. In some instances, other related but confidential changes may have prevented you from talking freely with everyone. There may well be any number of valid reasons, but that doesn't change the fact that they weren't prepared.

Others may be surprised and anxious, not sure what your change will mean for them. Is your new role a signal that they may lose their jobs? Were they passed over? Might they soon have their schedules or tasks changed? Are they losing a buddy or ally? Is your departure or arrival changing the dynamics of a group? Still others may be thrilled for you and wish they could have been part of the good news. These are real emotions (and concerns, maybe) that others have as they try to understand what your change means for them.

If you haven't prepared others for your change, then they can't begin adapting in ways that can support you. They won't know that they should, and they won't know how. Falling into this trap hurts them and, ultimately, hurts you and your transition.

RECOGNIZING THE RIPPLE EFFECTS

The collaborative, team-based approach prevalent in many organizations has given rise to more transitions, as individuals find themselves frequently moving between departments and joining cross-functional or ad hoc teams. Because we tend to focus most on our own situations, sometimes the amount of change and transition that others are working through isn't recognized within an organization, especially when it's experienced by those on the sidelines. One employee, Jack, described the extent of change he experienced in a single company, with little recognition or "permission" to feel anything about the effects.

In just five years, Jack reported to at least seven different managers across a variety of departments, projects, and environments. During this time he

- shifted from a team with a creative, "build it" focus to a functional team with a reputation for delivering the goods, with no real training on what the new role really meant;
- joined a work group with preexisting strong personalities and a difficult customer, then was expected to run the "traffic" of their complex interactions;
- joined a team with global reach, serving customers in remote locations; and
- became an on-location resource for a client, living temporarily in another state.

Even when Jack returned to his original boss, team, and job where he felt most comfortable, changes around him were still having an effect. Jack's boss took a leave of absence for medical reasons, a new temporary boss came in, and a coworker left the organization.

The frequent transitions sometimes caused Jack to begin a new transition before completely working through the implications of the previous one. Just as the excitement was ebbing and the first wave of uncertainty hit him, he was faced with a new transition. Being unable to arrive at the zone of Confidence and Transformation left him feeling as if he'd been left "disassembled" in terms of his confidence, effectiveness, relationships, and identity. He kept stopping partway, never getting to hit his stride and grow into a new identity.

Jack's experience suggests some advice to managers: Recognize the need both to prepare others for change and to support them during the process. Keep in mind that, whether the change is seen as good or bad, when an individual is going through a transition, both the organization and individual should acknowledge it and work together to make sure that people have the support that they need. Pay attention to the broader, more cumulative effects of change on others as they work through shifts and changes in routines or behavior, develop the skills they need, or reassess how to approach their work. Your change in role may feel like a single transition to you, but may be just one of many transitions for those on the sidelines.

EXPANDING YOUR IDENTITY

As many of you are most likely already aware, the demands of a more global and connected world can at times feel overwhelming. As we describe in each of the volumes of the *Leading from the Center* series, the challenges are many, complex, and dynamic. They are also intensified by roles that are changing more frequently. Transitions may be triggered by changes in work roles, but many managers are also opting to further their education while continuing to work full time—adding the role of student to their current identity.

One of the fastest-growing segments in higher education today is adults returning to school to better educate themselves, for either personal or professional reasons. According to the Education Resource Institute, the number of students aged 40 and older increased 235 percent between 1970 and 1993. Their reasons for returning to school vary: job obsolescence, advances in technology, pressure for a degree in their current job, better financial opportunities, and personal fulfillment.

Pursuing further education is a significant commitment, and being aware of some of the transition traps we describe here can also be helpful when considering blending this new role into one's identity. The Fuqua School of Business Executive MBA programs recognize this and attempt to ensure that potential applicants avoid the first trap by understanding exactly what they would be saying yes to. They describe the number of hours per week that potential students will be expected to devote to coursework above and beyond the time that they will spend in the classroom—completing readings, communicating with team members, and submitting assignments. Applicants are encouraged to consider not just how they may need to adapt to this change in role but also how this transition will impact those around them, such as coworkers, friends, and family. By understanding the commitment they are making, students are better able to prepare themselves and others for the change.

Because the Weekend Executive MBA students generally commute anywhere from five minutes to eight hours to and from the campus, that program also works to establish an extended support network for students' families. As Executive MBA students spend a considerable amount of their "free time" in class or working virtually with teammates, Fuqua invites partners and families to campus over one weekend to help them understand the demands placed on the students and to introduce them to other partners and families who are experiencing the same type of transition at home. Coming to campus to share the experience of a "class weekend" helps them better appreciate the challenges of this new role and also gives them an opportunity to meet all the people that their partner is talking about at home. Participation in the weekend helps them feel like they are in the loop on what's happening.

Last but not least, completing a degree often signals yet another transition. In many ways, new graduates are different people returning to a different place. Their experience has likely affected multiple layers of their identity as they incorporate new symbols (their degree), routines, skills, and knowledge. They perhaps have also changed beliefs about the ways that they interact with the world.

WHAT TO DO

Stop and think about your transition's impact on others or its significance for those around you. When you shift to a new role or project, those people with whom you interact on a daily basis have to transition as well. Do *they* understand what changes your new role will bring? Their attitudes and support will affect you and the results you can achieve. Your goal isn't necessarily to ensure that everyone agrees with or is happy with the change; rather, they need to be aware of it and clearly understand it. In other words, their eyes need to be open.

You will have to negotiate your new position in real time—not just the job you are doing but your relationships with other people. Starting this negotiation process before everything becomes "official" can make your transition faster and smoother.

Don't forget that transitions to new or shifting roles also require some degree of closure with your previous role. Don't allow "unfinished business" within your prior role to interfere with moving forward. For example, you might delay starting a new project until you reach a good milestone with an existing project. Or you may need to spend time and thought helping your replacement come up to speed. You may need to have a good-bye lunch with your team to thank them for working with you.

Understand the Connections

As you begin moving into your new role, you may need to manage new players, new geographies, new divisions, and new interactions. It's important to recognize all your connections and think about how you need to prepare those involved for your upcoming change.

A first step is to get a good sense of who needs to be aware of the change. You might want to create a diagram of your existing network of relationships, connections, and boundaries, then fill in what you think your new relationship network will (or needs to) look like. Consider including a wide range of people in your analysis:

- Team members who work directly with you
- Other teams
- Peers and colleagues
- Internal departments or divisions
- Internal or external clients, suppliers, competitors, and professional association members
- Others outside of work—family, friends, and social groups

Your goal is to see the range of relationships you have. Now consider who will be affected by your change directly and indirectly. Those directly affected will need to know about the change. Also ask yourself who you might, for political reasons, need to speak with ahead of time.

Have Frank Conversations

Once you have your diagram, you should have a sense of what to do next. Begin sharing information and negotiating with the following:

- *Your family.* Their first question may be whether they will have less time with you. Or if your new role means a relocation, change in schools, or change in routines. Does this mean you will be on call? Traveling? Working weekends? They need to be aware of and help you to consider what important personal commitments you need to meet and which you might need to let go.
- *Your friends, social groups, or volunteer organizations.* Just as you feel a commitment to family, you likely are connected to other groups. Anything new can take more of your time until you are comfortable in the role. For a while, you may simply feel the need to cut back on the number of optional activities. Your commitments may need to change to a different day or time because of new demands. For example, you may feel too overwhelmed to spend Monday nights with the regular football group.
- *Your current staff or project team.* They, too, will have many questions. You might put yourself in their shoes and consider what you would want to know. What changes will affect each of them? Is one of them ready to step up and assume leadership of the team? What unresolved problems are you leaving behind for them to deal with? Saying yes to a new opportunity may unintentionally send a signal that you no longer enjoy your current position or working with them. They may want to know how you will complete existing projects. Who will replace you—an outsider or a current team member? If the change is to take on another project, they may want to understand their roles and if the team is expanding.
- *Your new staff.* Any new boss typically signals a period of adjustment, even when the new manager is a welcome addition. Your staff may wonder about your style and your priorities and what impact you will have on them and their day-to-day activities. Your selection may coincide with the departure of another

manager who was respected and admired, or it may mean that another internal candidate was passed over. The sooner you can begin laying groundwork and building relationships with this group, the better. (Watkins, 2001)

- *Your new boss.* Did your new boss have the deciding vote in your selection? Would he or she have preferred someone with different qualities—more experience in the industry, more skill, more time on the job, or more education? How does this person approach her own role as a manager? Does your new boss understand the challenges that this new role or task presents for you, and is she available to coach you as you learn?

- *Your clients, suppliers, or vendors.* Are you the primary owner of the relationship? What does change mean for your interactions with them? Do you plan to introduce them to someone else who will be their main contact? How will that transition occur? Will you be more or less available than you have been in the past? Is decision-making responsibility shifting elsewhere?

Early on in your transition, you should be inviting others along on the ride. Letting them know what's coming and how it will affect all of you can help build a community of support rather than resistance. Then they can begin making their own choices and adjustments. You, too, will need to make adjustments as you go. If you don't make them soon enough, however, you can fall into the next trap: Not changing as much as you should.

CHAPTER FIVE

THE OLD SKILLS HAVE SERVED ME WELL

IN THIS CHAPTER

Expectations and the Real World ■ What about You?
■ The Skills That Got Me Here ■ What to Do

EXPECTATIONS AND THE REAL WORLD

Shifting roles and responsibilities are often accompanied by a need to change ourselves, and people generally expect that at some level. We may be realistic enough to know that everything won't be exactly the same, yet somehow we may envision that *others* will need to change and adapt, not us. Our expectations are often off the mark as to which elements will or won't change and to what extent. As a result, **we often ignore or underestimate our own need to change.**

As you begin a transition, you know it's not going to be just business as usual in a slightly different job. Yet early on, it may be hard to appreciate all that is or isn't shifting—and how far. The initial changes associated with a transition tend to be more visible and perhaps more anticipated, and most of them are associated with outer layers of identity that we described in Chapter 1:

- *Status.* Titles, peer groups, committees, or a "place at the table"

- *People.* New relationships, changes to old relationships, more people, or a larger network
- *Physical locations.* Office, department, building, or geography
- *Schedules and routines.* Meetings, check-ins, or social events
- *Work culture.* Team dynamics, division, group, or location culture
- *Accountability.* Shift in focus, new or additional deliverables, priorities, or responsibility for results

Problems begin when our own expectations, others' expectations, and reality are at odds with one another—expectations around key elements such as competency, authority, or acknowledgment. For example, let's say you have a new title—you're now a full partner instead of an associate—and you have expectations about what goes along with that change. You may expect that people will regard you as a more senior member of the firm, you'll get a nicer office, or you'll be invited to participate in strategic committees. What you find instead is that for now, you sit in the same office, interact with many of the same people, and in general, not much seems to have changed. You still have to get the same work done, and you're not even sure that others realize that a change has occurred for you. There is more "business as usual" than you expected. You wonder if you should be doing anything differently and, if so, what?

On the other hand, the opposite situation can be just as difficult. You may have been asked to add more responsibility to your current position. You aren't very familiar with the new area but plan to devote some time to learning quickly more about this product line, division, or project team. Instead, you find yourself immediately expected to take ownership of this new part of your role—direct reports are knocking on your door, customers are calling your number, and your e-mail is filling with new meeting requests. Others are looking to you to make decisions and make progress. You sit in the chair, so you are expected to know what to do. In this case, there is less "business as usual" than you expected. Just as in the first example, you suspect you should be doing some things differently but, if so, what?

WHAT ABOUT YOU?

As external conditions change around you, what about your own need to change? You may have been the star performer on your old team, but that status may not translate or carry over to the new role. Your relationships may have been well established and comfortable with your previous peers, but you may no longer be collaborating with them. The reality is that your working world has shifted. How you adapt will be critical.

A lot can feel new in a changing role, and a lot can also feel the same. Yet people in transition often underestimate the scope and scale of change that they themselves will need to make. Fundamentally, they understand that they need to change, but they don't carry this thought through into action. They get trapped in their existing ways of thinking and acting and either do nothing or don't make *enough* of a change to become as effective as possible in their new role.

Consider Jackie. She was a section manager in a department store for many years, running the bedding and bath department directly and overseeing fine china, crystal, and housewares as well. When the overall store manager left, Jackie got promoted. At first, everything was fine. She knew all the department managers and thought most were really strong, so she didn't want to interfere in their work. She kept an eye on the sales and inventory numbers, walked around, held a weekly managers' meeting, and answered letters from customers. She made sure the store was operating smoothly, in the same way she'd made sure the departments in her section ran smoothly, but didn't recognize that managing the store also meant being part of a larger system. She didn't interact with her regional manager enough, nor did she actively reinforce or promote the new direction corporate wanted to take. Jackie was focused on her store and her managers and didn't change the scope of her routines to include the organization beyond the store. Ultimately, she had a series of uncomfortable meetings and a poor performance appraisal, until she understood what her boss expected her to do, and then shifted her identity beyond being a great section manager. She finally grew into the mantle of store manager, adopting a more strategic focus instead of just monitoring the day to day.

Jackie isn't that different from other people in transition we've known. It can be hard to change yourself. This may be because people in transition are so focused on external changes—results, budgets, other people—that they overlook the extent to which they need to adapt their own behavior or interactions. Nor do they start their identity shifts early enough. For instance, people tend to overestimate how far their past experiences and accomplishments will take them. They have always been successful, always managed to get the job done. They assume that the skills that have served them well thus far will continue to serve them well, so they continue doing more of the same.

However, previous accomplishments, skills, or talents may not be as relevant in this new place. It may be great that you can write clear and detailed project status reports. However, in your new position, you find you are expected to deliver two-minute status updates face-to-face and field rapid-fire questions from the group. In this case, the scope of your new responsibilities requires you to communicate and interact in a very different way than before. Your writing skills won't be much help in establishing your credibility or influencing this group.

Not only might your strengths not be as useful, they could become a weakness. Your preference for selecting a single "right" solution and then systemically working to implement it could backfire if you are now in a situation where quick idea generation and prototyping are the norm. Your level of expertise in a particular area may make you more prone to micromanaging people who perform that same task within your new team. Be available to coach or offer input without taking over. (Watkins, 2003)

Change involves not just the new capabilities you need, but sometimes it also involves changes to tasks you've done before. For example, you may have been using e-mail and voicemail for years, but this new role has suddenly tripled the number of messages that you receive each day. You may have facilitated hundreds of meetings but not with a cross-functional group that spans four time zones. You may need to take stock not just of what is clearly new but also some of the more subtle modifications in your tasks, behavior, or routines.

Finally, people may not just underestimate their own need to change but completely ignore it. They may assume that because they

"The old tricks, young fellow, have served me well."

are in a leadership position, it's up to those around them to do the changing: "I know how I like to work, and my team should cater to my preferred style." Some may, incorrectly, assume that their transition really involves other people accommodating the new boss.

This trap is a problem, because underestimating the changes you need to make means you're not adjusting as much or as fast as you should be. The need won't go away, and you will still have to make those adjustments. Slowing down your transition means it will take you that much longer until you are humming along effectively in your new position.

THE SKILLS THAT GOT ME HERE

Wilhelm was thrilled to be selected as the new factory manager where he had been the quality manager for the past six years. Wilhelm was excited by the possibilities that lay in front of him: Increased supervisory responsibilities and decision-making power as well as the possibility to move to other locations, as many factory managers did in his organization.

His penchant for accuracy in data collection and monitoring key performance indicators in the production process had proven to be real strengths as quality manager. In particular, Wilhelm was proud of his group's "five nines" performance over the past three years. In his production lines, his crews had managed an average 99.999 percent at or above minimum specifications for quality standards for outgoing product. He had implemented several new procedures and quality assessments that were now widely used across the company—laudable accomplishments that had played no small part, he was sure, in his selection as factory manager.

He felt this promotion would provide opportunities for similar levels of process refinement within the building, and Wilhelm was eager to get started and demonstrate his competence. His confidence was high, as he got his calendar set with process reviews with each section head in the factory. Wilhelm had built good relationships with his colleagues in the other sections, and he looked forward to having the authority to convince them of the benefits of his approach to process management.

What happened, however, over the ensuing weeks was anything but simple. Despite the logic of Wilhelm's plan, the section heads were slow to respond, or they just ignored his e-mail requests. He took great care in sending the full details of his plan for process management, expecting to see his production managers, supply managers, and line managers respond with an implementation plan. Why weren't they responding?

Also, he struggled to respond to five times as many e-mails and phone calls as he used to get on topics with which he was unfamiliar. His organizational skills and routines worked well for a small scope of responsibility but were less effective here. How was he supposed to know what to do about the local media request to interview floor workers on their working conditions? Should he ask his administrative assistant what the former factory manager would have done?

Making matters worse, corporate was pushing a new set of training requirements for different job positions within the organization, and they needed a compliance plan from him in two weeks. He had over 350 employees in 14 different jobs affected by this initiative and no local human resources representative.

Wilhelm suddenly felt isolated in his position, and he retreated to the privacy of his office more and more, choosing to create implementation plans for the department heads to use. He felt comfortable in that task and thought perhaps that would bring them around to see the benefit of his ideas. And, quietly, Wilhelm hoped that the growing silence between him and his former colleagues would be at last broken with this effort to produce a plan for them.

But mostly, Wilhelm just felt unprepared. He had a nagging feeling that he didn't know what he didn't know, and that others should be helping him more than they were. He was discovering that there was much more to developing relationships with the people that surrounded him (external community, corporate office, internal colleagues) and that his finely tuned quality management skills were practically useless. He realized that just working harder wasn't the answer; he needed to work smarter. New routines to manage interacting with more people and new approaches toward his role in leading them would help him be less overwhelmed.

WHAT TO DO

Assume You Have Something to Learn

Your previous skills got you here, but what skills will take you to the next level? Enter a learning mode, rather than assuming that you already have what it takes to get the job done. You've been given this chance because you have potential and the core qualities to succeed—not necessarily because you are already fully developed for the new role. You need to build the capabilities necessary to manage your new tasks effectively and handle the old ones in their new form.

Get Help Early and from Multiple Sources

Don't let your desire to appear competent and confident undermine your learning. A common mistake people make, especially when the new opportunity is a promotion, is thinking that they are expected to begin with the same competence and style of someone more experienced and established in that role. Being tagged for a new challenge—large or small—doesn't mean that the company believes you currently have all of the capabilities you will need, just that management believes you have some of the necessary core capabilities, as well as the ability to enhance them. You also are not expected to do the job in exactly the same way as your role models. People can be equally effective using very different approaches.

Inquiry and reflection don't indicate a lack of ability but send a signal that you know enough to know that you don't have all the answers and are seeking to learn from others. There is a saying: "Fake it until you make it." There is some truth to that. You have to assume the role even though you don't know how to do it fully; you have to project your willingness to accept the responsibility. Eventually, though, you will need to "make it." The question is how much difficulty you'll put yourself through in the process. Saving face and not admitting that you're having trouble may be the wrong approach. Others see that you're on a learning curve, so it's not as though they don't know, and not admitting it delays the cavalry from coming in and helping you. Look across your network (and beyond) and assume that everyone has something to teach you—from immediate team members, to peers, to senior leaders.

Think about How You Spend Your Day

Consider how you spend your time, with whom you interact, what you need to accomplish, and how effective you are in accomplishing it. Have you made adjustments in all of these areas? If not, why not? You may be falling into the trap.

- *Time.* Understand what time means and the value of it in your new world. What should you be spending your time on? To manage your time effectively, you need to understand where it's gone by the end of the day—not the schedule that you had planned on paper, but what actually happened. That's not to say that you need to devote as little time as possible to each task, but that you need to allocate the right amount of time needed to be effective at the most important things, even if it's a large piece of your day. That may mean an hour of unplanned time on the phone with a key customer. Allocate your time like a scarce resource that cannot be replaced. (Drucker, 2002)

- *Routines.* What routines will help you in your new role? You may need to reflect on how you get work done. You may need to change the pattern of your day or week. For example, if you took on a project with an outside company, do you have a routine in place for checking in with your counterparts there? For staying current on their industry? If your new team members are morning people, having a lunch meeting will be less effective than having coffee together at 8:00 AM. You may need to shift returning phone calls to later in the day.

  You may need to create new routines. For example, your new role may involve budgeting and purchasing, areas for which you weren't responsible in the past. What routines have you established to track expenses and materials and to do the required reports?

- *Relationships.* Begin building relationships before you need them. Connect to direct reports, peers, and others across the organization. You may not understand all the connections or implications of the relationships yet, but you need to get started.

Leverage Your Learning

You may have a lot to learn, but you can't and shouldn't try to learn everything overnight.

- Find a new coach or mentor, or call your current mentor more often and ask for guidance in your learning process.

- Of all the things you don't know, identify the critical knowledge or skills that will give you the most leverage and pursue those first.
- Which parts of your learning will come through trial and feedback, which from experience? Think about what opportunities will offer the best environment for learning, enabling you to try new knowledge and skills with some degree of support and air cover.
- Make time for reflection and adjustment. Think through the implications of what you've learned and how you can apply that knowledge in this situation.

Over time, you can shift your identity and skills to match your new role. Transition takes time, willingness, and help. As we take on new behaviors, though, letting go of what we've done before can be hard. Not realizing how much we'll need to change is one trap; not being willing to let go is another. That's where we turn next: when holding onto the past prevents us from moving forward.

CHAPTER SIX

I'M HAVING AN IDENTITY CRISIS

IN THIS CHAPTER

Letting Go, Holding On ▪ Your Comfort Zone
▪ We're in This Together ▪ What to Do

LETTING GO, HOLDING ON

You might feel both helpless and hopeless without a sense of a "map" for the journey. Confusion is the hallmark of a transition. To rebuild both your inner and outer world is a major project.

Anne Grant, Ph.D.

In times of stress, we have a tendency to hold on tight to what we know, what we're good at, and what feels comfortable, especially those strengths that have produced success in the past. During a transition, much is already in flux; people may hesitate to add to the chaos and instead look for something stable to hold on to while they sort through what's changing. In a transition, many people find themselves holding on to their former identity—**not able to let go of what they do well long enough to learn something new.** They may hold on to some or all of their previous beliefs, skills, and habits, even though these are no longer useful to creating success.

57

As parts of their role are evolving, they may find that they feel out of alignment. People in transition may not feel as confident and effective in what they are doing as they used to. They may question their natural abilities, their values and behaviors, the relevance of their skills and expertise, the power of their authority, or the value of their network. Something they always prided themselves at being good at—a particular expertise—seems to be unimportant or less valued now.

Transitions can strike at the heart, particularly for people who have a hard time reshaping their identity. To the extent that their professional role makes up part of their identity, a transition can threaten them at a very personal and intimate level. It can throw into question how they see themselves fundamentally. Part of this trap is not letting go of a piece of their identity. Yet, until they start to see themselves differently, they cannot assume their new role fully. They are holding themselves back by not letting go.

Sometimes, transitions can be difficult because no one signals a change to others, so they may not allow you to let go. There may be no announcement about your new responsibilities or authority, no welcoming party, no new office or perks, and no honeymoon period. You may be expected to take on important tasks with little fanfare and just get it done. In this case, you are in the middle of a transition, but others may not offer any recognition that something has changed. They may expect you to behave and operate just as you have been. That makes it even more critical that you be proactive in avoiding this trap.

Other times, transitions are difficult because the outer symbols are there, but your inner feelings of confidence or competency may be out of line with how others see you or with what they expect. In other words, putting on the "hat" doesn't mean you feel competent enough to do the job. For example, you may be part of a new team or group without really feeling like one of them—you may even feel like an imposter. You may feel out of place because the others at the table have established relationships with one another and a connection to the group's history. You haven't shifted your sense of identity to include being a member of this new group and, as a result, you may hold back and send unconscious signals that you think you don't belong.

"You're five now, Lance. You've got to let go of four."

When your uncertainty about your evolving role increases, you may focus too much energy on hanging on to the comfort of the familiar instead of putting the right amount of energy into adapting. For example, a colleague may seek your input on a customer problem that you would have handled previously. It may very well be helpful and appropriate for your coworker to seek your perspective, as you're well acquainted with the individuals involved or the historical background. However, it doesn't help either of you for you to step back into that prior role—directly contacting the customer, attending a planning meeting, or coordinating your previous team's plan of action.

Recognize that, just as you need to build your own skills and knowledge, those who may be assuming parts of your previous role are going through a similar transition. They may not immediately know the answer as you would. They may not have as extensive a network. Don't base your own reluctance to let go on their inexperience. Yes, they may need support and coaching, but the work will certainly go on without you.

Although reconnecting with the familiar may temporarily bolster your confidence and sense of identity, in the long run, this does nothing to help develop the capabilities that you and others need for the future. You will have to learn how to integrate yourself effectively within each new or shifting role, priority, project, or group of people. Each integration or transition refines small pieces of your identity.

Understanding what aspects of your identity to hold onto and what aspects to let go of is key. You may be in a situation where you can't completely let go of your previous identity—you may have been asked to split your time between two departments, for example, or to hand off some of your tasks to others to make room for a time-consuming new responsibility. Even so, if you don't make the best choices in creating the right mix for your new identity, you can create even more problems:

- *Leaving no room for others to grow.* If you continually step in to save the day, others can't learn by experience.
- *Leaving no room for yourself to grow.* You have a gap in the skills and knowledge you need for your new tasks. Focusing on previous responsibilities can leave your new responsibilities partly undone or unattended. Your time and energy are resources you need to manage.
- *Imposing on others.* If you are distracted, someone else will have to reach in and take care of what you leave undone, or you just live with lackluster results.

YOUR COMFORT ZONE

In a number of coaching assignments, Kirby Warren (former dean of Columbia's Graduate School of Business) and Bob Fulmer

(Distinguished Visiting Professor of Strategy at Pepperdine University) have seen individuals who had difficulty letting go of their old identity during transitions. The following composite represents some of the issues they have observed with this challenge.

George Baker had just been given the promotion of his dreams. After a series of successes in sales management, he was offered the position of vice president of marketing for the Southwest. Throughout his career, George had been successful in developing strong relationships with key clients while motivating and developing the sales reps who worked for him. Despite George's lack of direct experience in marketing administration, his boss chose George for the position because he had been a valuable member of the marketing team and demonstrated the potential to grow into the VP role. He had also been an effective coach and mentor for Tammy Evans, who seemed ready to step into George's old position.

After six months, there was growing concern that neither individual seemed to be doing well in the new positions. George had not really stepped up to the broader aspects of his new job and seemed to be spending most of his time addressing crises back in the sales arena. His outer identity layers had changed as he assumed the title and the office, but adjusting the inner layers was proving harder.

George confided to his boss that he was concerned about Tammy's failure to "grow into her new job," and that he was considering removing her from it: "The problem is, I just don't know where I can move her now. It may be best to just let her go, as it would be very awkward for her and those around her to move her back a level. She lacks a sense of priorities, and I'm spending much more time than I should be trying to keep her out of trouble. She's spending too much time in meetings with her people and not enough with key customers. Several key clients have told me that they haven't seen her in several months."

George's boss was wise enough to understand that George was holding onto his sales identity because he was confident of his abilities there but unsure how to approach his new tasks. Unfortunately, this meant he wasn't letting Tammy learn her new job. His constant retreat backwards left her no room to grow.

A forceful and direct approach would have exacerbated George's insecurity and done nothing to build the skills and knowledge he needed—like throwing a person who hasn't learned how to swim in the deep end of the pool. Instead, his boss offered support to help George reorient his view of the role and how he believed he should approach it. First, recalling that George had successfully designed a sales compensation system for his region, she asked him to develop a new compensation plan for the marketing organization and insisted that he have a draft on her desk in three weeks. This focused George's attention in an area where he felt competent and provided him with a chance to start proving himself in his new area. Second, she paired George with a more experienced colleague who was able to coach him in additional aspects of this level of leadership. As he became more comfortable with his new skills, he also began to consider himself as the vice president of marketing for the first time. As he focused more on his own developing knowledge and beliefs, achieving some small successes and receiving additional support, he stopped obsessing about the fact that Tammy was using a different, but ultimately successful, approach to his old job.

WE'RE IN THIS TOGETHER

Occasionally, your identity shift may occur as a result of a larger company initiative that affects a number of people. Not only are you facing a personal transition to a new or changing role, but you have the added complexity of making this shift as part of a team. For example, one global company took on the strategic challenge of building a Learning and Education Division by using a blend of successful internal executives and newly hired learning professionals. The idea was that an internal-external mix and a line-learning mix would allow the team to succeed at a faster pace. Most in the newly formed group were executives taken out of their comfort zone and asked to become learning consultants. In a matter of a few days, they went from respected experts to novices. The result was predictable—a new team of angry, unfocused, and ambivalent people.

To help this new team with their transition, the chief learning officer brought them together for a three-week intensive boot camp.

When the team first arrived, everyone was holding on to a previous identity. They didn't yet know how to think of themselves or what value they would have. They showed up for the meeting with critical questions: What am I here for? How am I supposed to do this? During the three weeks, they slowly acclimated to their new role and began the process of constructing their new identities. They spent time as a group discussing the importance of the challenge and the change that was in store for them. Once back on the job, that process continued. They created new routines, interacted with a new group of peers, and began to see themselves differently. They learned new skills, knowledge, and expertise as they explored the area they were charged with leading. As time passed and the project moved forward, their inner layers of identity underwent changes. They began to believe deeply that education was a valuable strategic lever that would take the company forward.

WHAT TO DO

This is a time for assessing and building the capabilities that you need and for building new relationships and negotiating the expectations of peers, bosses, and others.

Assess Your Gaps

Getting comfortable with your transition requires assessing and then filling the gaps that may be tempting you to hold onto your previous identity. Ask yourself:

- What routines or behaviors would better align with your new role? Which are now less useful?
- What skills and knowledge would serve you well but today present a challenge and need to be developed?
- Do you need to change how you think of yourself as a professional? How you approach and interact with others?
- What are you willing to do to close those gaps?

Develop a Start, Stop, or Continue List

Two main ways to close the capability gaps are to develop your own capabilities and to access others' expertise. Focus on your skills first, then on what others may take on for you.

When your role changes, you should leave behind some tasks and skills, adopt new ones, and continue to use and improve on others. Being clear which is which helps you focus your attention and transition more quickly. After you have assessed your strengths and development areas as they relate to this role, make a plan. Decide what you will need to *start, stop,* or *continue* doing to help you make a successful transition.

If you didn't do your old job well, you wouldn't be where you are now. Which skills and talents that got you here will also serve you in this new space? Which tasks are more effectively delegated to others? Where are your own gaps? Consider the start, stop, or continue adjustments for the manufacturing worker who moves into a line supervisor position, the salesperson who becomes a sales manager, the physician who moves from a private practice to group practice, or a faculty member who shifts from instructor to administrator.

The new roles require a different set of capabilities, focus, and interactions. For example, in your life as a college professor, you might be something of a lone wolf, your success primarily dependent on your individual efforts at research, publishing, and teaching. On the other hand, if you're an administrator, your focus shifts, and you learn that running a department can't be done alone. You have to work with others to refine budgets, hire and develop new staff, redesign curriculum changes, and plan strategic direction. It can be tough to spend less time or no time at all on the parts of your previous role that you enjoyed and did well. Assess what new tasks will require your attention, which tasks are better suited for others, and what tasks you might continue to participate in. Keep in mind that you may have to find greater satisfaction in new achievements and label your own success differently.

For example, let's say you were a public relations associate for a multinational organization. However, you have just started a new job as a PR director for a large nonprofit. A stop, start, or continue list for you might look like this:

- Start or improve team administration, creating supporting materials for fundraising and giving keynote speeches in place of writing press releases
- Stop (delegate) how to look up newspaper clippings in online databases
- Continue to leverage technical knowledge of communications and marketing fields

Once you have sorted out your own stop, start, or continue, consider what others can contribute. In the previous example, if a skill such as researching via online databases is needed only occasionally, rely on others to provide that capability.

Reflect on How You See Yourself

In a transition, people need to begin seeing themselves in the new role, taking it on as part of themselves. If they don't, instead continuing to cling to an outdated view, they cannot succeed. For example, someone who began a career as a welder, then becomes manager of a $10 million project, can't grab a torch and fix a problem. This person can't continue to see himself as a welder first; the role of project manager means he needs to assign someone else to fix welding problems. He needs to build professional pride and self-image around being a manager. If you find yourself holding on to a former identity, consider these questions:

- What is holding you back?
- Are you becoming who you want to be?
- Are you right for this role?

You must stay true to yourself as you undergo the identity shift to your new role, and you need to know what makes you comfortable—what you will and will not do.

Be Clear on Accountability

You have a nice list of activities you will stop doing. Some tasks or skills aren't needed for your team's work. Others may be, but you aren't the person who should do them. You need to speak to those you work with and be clear on who is doing what.

- Negotiate and clearly communicate with others what areas you will continue to be responsible for, which you will let go of, and what tasks you will assume. You'll likely have some of each, but the list isn't always clear and may change over time. For example, if you are remaining in your current role but taking on new areas of responsibility or additional projects, how will you make room for your new responsibilities? Are you reassigning or delegating some tasks?
- Create a realistic transition time line in which you gradually shift the appropriate pieces to other staff or assume accountability for new pieces. For example, you may hand off some customers to other managers right away. Others you might hand over more slowly to protect key relationships. Think about what role you'll play in advising and assisting your replacement, and figure out who is responsible for that transition plan. When considering how fast to transition out of the old role, also consider how quickly you will be accountable for your new area. There are limits to how much you can do, so be realistic as you take on and give up work.

Consider what you need to stop, start, or continue doing. Also, consider when those shifts should happen. Although assessing your skill gap or action list is mostly an individual task, remedying any missing abilities or insufficiencies requires help from others. How do you get the support you need when you need it? Transitions are not a solo event. Those who think they are will fall into our next trap: working without a support network.

CHAPTER SEVEN

WHERE'S MY SAFETY NET?

IN THIS CHAPTER

Too Narrow a Network ■ No Foundation of Support
■ Are You Leaving Your Network Behind? ■ What to Do

One of the recurring themes in making a transition is that to be successful, you do not go through it alone. You need to bring other people along with you and get new people involved. A typical trap is **not connecting with the right mix of people who will be able to support you in this process.** If your new staff resents you, if you don't have an expert you can call when a crisis erupts, or if you can't get the resources you need for your new project, then you haven't built the right network of support to succeed. As you assume a new role or experience changes in your current responsibilities, you should expand your network and start to build a foundation of acceptance before making significant changes.

That's not to say that you should remain inactive while you develop your network. When Microsoft acquired Groove Networks in early 2005, its founder Ray Ozzie was named a chief technology officer at Microsoft. He later commented that some executives had advised him that Microsoft was a big company and that he should "get to know it for a year or so" before deciding where to focus and how to proceed. He reported that he followed that advice—for about two weeks. Then he spent the next several months meeting with people across the company to learn more about what they were working on, have conversations, and compile his thoughts on simple and compelling software services that "just work." His collected ideas resulted in a seven-page memo titled "The Internet Services Disruption" that cited missed opportunities and named competitors—a tactic designed to both educate the troops and stir them to action. (Lohr, *New York Times*, December 11, 2005)

TOO NARROW A NETWORK

During their initial excitement about the opportunity they've agreed to, people often focus more on themselves than on others—will they personally enjoy this change, will they be effective, do they have the right skills? Because they feel confident in their own capabilities, their thoughts don't immediately turn to the new groups with which they will interact and the relationships they need to build. Even as their excitement begins to wane and doubt sets in about their ability to make this transition successfully, people may still think that their existing network will be sufficient. Here are some common assumptions and mistakes around adapting one's network:

- *Slow to begin conversations.* Because they don't really understand their new role well, people may not begin conversations with the right people soon enough. Their existing network doesn't match their new needs, but they are slow to realize that. A weak network means they may not have access to other groups, resources, perspectives, or personal support when the need arises.

- *Don't anticipate beyond obvious resources.* They may not consider the new categories of resources that they will need for their new role or task. A new CEO may not have an attorney to call for advice. A director may not have a finance person who can answer tactical questions. Changing roles may require access to different kinds of expertise, and some people don't assess their new needs.

- *Fail to use peer resources.* People often forget that peers are a wonderful resource. They aren't usually competitors, are generally on the same side as you, and they sit in similar situations. Their point of reference is close, yet their experience is different enough, making them a rich resource.
- *Reach out too late.* People may delay reaching out and expanding their network. Your first interaction with people who can help should be *before* you need them—build a relationship before asking for assistance.
- *Don't extend far enough.* Finally, look more broadly and build a network of relationships beyond the boundaries of your own organization. In *The Third Opinion*, Sai-nicole Joni explains how everyone from senior executives to first-level managers can benefit from a diverse group of advisors, experts, mentors, or confidants. This externally positioned inner circle of advisors can often offer a more trustworthy, loyal, and unbiased perspective. (Joni, 2004)

Failing to navigate and build a network of relationships may lead you to a point where you do feel all alone, and in many ways you are. However, you can't be successful alone.

NO FOUNDATION OF SUPPORT

As we discussed in Chapter 4, people will respond differently to you in your new or altered role. Some may be thrilled and jump right in with you. Others may be more cautious, waiting to see if you'll succeed or fail. They withhold judgment and may also withhold support. During your transition, you will need to shift your identity not only in your own eyes but in others' eyes as well. You need to build a foundation of acceptance, helping people accept you in your new role, before you become effective.

Although it's true that we build our identity, authority, and credibility over time through our actions and relationships, it's also true that early, successful interactions are very important, as people tend to form impressions very quickly. Early interactions shape later ones, because they set the tone and begin to shape the boundaries of your relationships. People will observe you—how you work and with whom—for clues about what kind of leader you will be. The more limited the interactions, the more people will infer from each one. Poor early interactions can harden people's opinions, and it may take a long time to recover and regain their support.

For example, Marcia was to take over a software programming group in a few weeks. She sent an e-mail to her soon-to-be team, asking each of them to describe who they were and what role they played. She continued that she wanted all of them to explain their view of the software field, because she'd not worked in software programming before. Deadline: end of the week. That was all. Symbolically, Marcia's first act set the tone for what was to come. She made a demand of people who didn't yet report to her and set a tone that said, "Be prepared for an inquisition." This approach made her future team wary of her interpersonal and leadership skills. It didn't set up a foundation for acceptance or support. In fact, after a few months, she was moved to lead a different team, having failed to make a successful transition.

ARE YOU LEAVING YOUR NETWORK BEHIND?

As a young, high-potential manager, Ricardo had been working in corporate communications, supporting a line of business. As a direct report to an executive vice president, Ricardo was responsible for marketing materials, internal communications, presentations, etc. After a few years, he was asked to focus on a particular division—conducting market research, developing initiatives for the division, and identifying several product innovations customers wanted. Due to the high visibility of the job, Ricardo established a very strong network at the senior executive level in the company.

The high visibility of Ricardo's job led to an opportunity to move from a corporate position to a line role in the division. Flattery and confidence from others about this shift made it seem like a natural transition for him. He had very little trepidation about making the leap into managing customers—and doing so successfully. He thought, "I'm a smart human being. I'm well connected. I can take on anything that's thrown at me."

A couple of months into the job, Ricardo realized that he had failed to consider one very important factor when he made this transition. By taking on the line job, Ricardo no longer interacted regularly with the company's executive leadership. Because he reported into the division hierarchy, he no longer had direct access to the executives in Milan. He was hearing wisps that he was standoffish, didn't fit in, and was "stealing" people's customer relationships. He needed to start connecting with "the locals" quickly.

To make matters worse, just as Ricardo began to reach out to his new colleagues, there was a change in executive leadership. Many of his previous advocates and mentors were either assigned to different regional positions or let go. This shift in leadership had an adverse effect on Ricardo—in the span of a couple of months, he had a new boss and new colleagues, and his internal network evaporated. Rumors of layoffs were starting to swirl, and he no longer felt protected. His belief that being connected to the small executive group was good enough was shattered; a broader and more extensive network was proving to be more useful.

After narrowly escaping being laid off, Ricardo needed to regroup. Given the time he had spent at headquarters, he had a wide (though not deep) base of contacts with people in all parts of the company. He began to reach out to those around him through what he called "issue sensing." Ricardo used informal communication channels as a means to listen in, learn more about what was occurring throughout the company, and gain a better sense of the types of issues colleagues were facing. These informal avenues gave him an easy way to initiate conversations with others locally and around the company and to rebuild his network. Within nine months, he overheard that he was the person to go to if you needed help working with a customer.

As a result of this transition, Ricardo was able to add several facets to his identity. He realized he not only needed marketing and customer relationship skills to succeed but company relationships, too. As a result of connecting more broadly, he has become more visible to others and is seen as a key resource across the company. As he approaches his next transition, a stronger network of support will be ready to help him.

WHAT TO DO

Expand Your Network

Part of a transition is acknowledging change. In the previous chapter, we talked about recognizing changes in your own identity. You cannot stay static when taking on new challenges, and neither can your relationships. Your ability to get results is largely dependent on the quality of relationships you have. You will have different needs than before, and your existing network may not be able to help you. Ask yourself if you have the right mix or amount of the following:

- *Personal support.* Your family and friends are important to keep you grounded and to offer emotional support. However, you may find you need additional help, occasionally in unusual ways. For example, a vice president of finance for a small company was working long hours. She quickly learned that by the time she got home and she and her daughter made dinner and cleared away the dishes, they didn't have much time to talk. She decided to let someone else make dinner; she and her daughter began eating out twice a week at local restaurants. They used the time between ordering and eating to catch up and ate the leftovers on other nights. The VP was able to buy some support, loosening the constraints on her time.
- *Coaches or mentors.* You may need some help in developing the confidence and competence to do your new role. Can your existing coaches or mentors provide enough feedback, support, and guidance in the new skills and challenges you face? Do you have role models—people who are already comfortable in this role or a similar one—that you can observe and emulate as you work your way through the transition?
- *Opportunities to connect with new people.* Reach out to build new connections or change existing relationships. Invite someone to lunch. Attend a professional group meeting and introduce yourself to someone you don't know. Have your mentor or boss act as a liaison to a distant peer in your organization or in a cus-

tomer group. Sometimes you have to engineer "excuses" to interact with others.

The key to avoiding the trap of finding yourself without a sufficient network of support is to be proactive in reaching out, including people in your transition *before* you need their help. Be inviting. Be open. Make an effort to listen.

Build a Solid Foundation

Being accepted in your new role is all about relationships and impressions. You need to convince people that you are a good bet and they should work with you. How?

- *Get people engaged with you.* Part of this is being clear about what you need and getting people excited to provide it. Tell a good story that captures people's imagination. (See our book, *Influencing and Collaborating for Results*, for more detail.) Mend fences if you need to. Have others help you spread the word—indirect contact can be very effective. Be inviting and share the credit.
- *Demonstrate competence.* You can do this many ways. Do your homework, that is, be very prepared and knowledgeable about your area, customers, industry, and so on. Continue to do research and stay up-to-date. Competence is demonstrated both by sharing what you do know when it's appropriate and by admitting when you don't know something but are eager to learn.
- *Build credibility and trust.* Follow through on what you say you're going to do, and others will reciprocate. Have expertise that others know about and can rely on. Begin to reach out and be helpful to people, building a reservoir of goodwill so it's there when you need it most.
- *Consider and adapt your leadership style.* Think about the environment in which you'll be working. Your present style may not match, and you may need to shift your behavior. For example, where and how do you focus—on results and getting tasks done, on developing people and building connections,

on having a professional and dispassionate demeanor, on engaging in social talk, on using authority to persuade, or on developing personal relationships to request action? Recall Marcia from earlier in this chapter: Her style set up a barrier before she even met her team.

- *Create some supportive routines.* All of these changes to the way that you work won't come naturally. Creating routines helps remind you to continue building your foundation, even when it's easier to get caught up in the day-to-day work and neglect this important aspect of your transition. Find a time twice a week to reach out to a peer just to catch up. Put a standing appointment on your calendar with yourself—10 minutes to reflect on the week past and the week ahead, or 30 minutes to exercise, or a reminder bell to work on a particular skill or behavior change.

- *Focus on small, early wins.* Nothing breeds success like success. Sometimes you will need to get a few small wins to build confidence before you can tackle your larger aims. For example, Evan wanted to get people in his company to share best practices. He began with a "brown bag" talk once a month for his team and a team in a different division. They used video over the Internet to connect the two lunch rooms. In just a few months, the two teams had learned so much from one another, and generated positive word of mouth, that three other teams began joining the brown bag talks. Evan was able to secure permission to continue them and got a budget to provide dessert for attendees at all sites. The trial run with two teams succeeded, so he could then expand the reach.

Building support is critical to your success. You cannot succeed alone, and others may surprise you with their willingness to help. Let them be a part of your success. If you isolate yourself, you may slip deeper into uncertainty and doubt your ability to perform in this new position. You may find yourself in the next trap: thinking you have no choice.

CHAPTER EIGHT

WHAT CHOICE DO I HAVE?

IN THIS CHAPTER

Feeling Trapped ■ Seeing Your Options
■ A Decision to Adapt and Move Forward ■ A Decision to Exit
■ What to Do

FEELING TRAPPED

You may have been caught in a zone of increasing doubt for some time, gradually losing confidence in your ability to be successful, thinking that you may have made a mistake in taking on this challenge, or feeling alone and missing your old support network. In many cases, when people feel out of control or off-kilter, their uncertainty and doubt can grow into something akin to terror. They took the job or agreed to the special assignment—perhaps falling prey to some of the early transition traps—and now fear that they can't pull it off. They worry that they might become unemployed or unemployable. **In the midst of this, they often can't see and understand that they *do* have choices.**

These doubts and fears really put the *trapped* in transition traps. People hit this low point and may be depressed or afraid. Feeling effective and comfortable in this new role didn't come as quickly as they would have liked or as smoothly as they'd hoped. There may be small signs of success, but those signs may not be enough to encourage them to keep trying. And they may feel as if they are running out of time. It just feels bad—not feeling entirely competent and comfortable yet not knowing necessarily what to do differently.

Having gotten this far, people in transition tend to see only the need to do what they promised: "What choice do I have? I took on this project and need to see it through, although it's killing me. I can't disappoint the team or my boss. I asked my family to make sacrifices. I just need to put my head down and push forward." The *real* trap is in continuing to flounder, believing you don't have a choice other than to continue, and slowly either becoming resentful or feeling hopeless. If you don't make a conscious choice when you're in a tough spot, your transition will stall.

"Look, I have my misgivings, too, but what choice do we have except to stay the course?"

SEEING YOUR OPTIONS

In reality, people always have a choice, although some options are decidedly more attractive than others. The first step is to understand that any choice will require some action on your part. A common mistake that people make at this point is to do nothing, essentially choosing not to make a choice. This inability or reluctance to see other options will only keep you trapped and prolong the pain. Alternatives to staying in your current state are to figure out how to make it work here or to leave this role behind and become successful elsewhere.

The Decision to Continue and Make It Work

In choosing this path, you're actually making two decisions—first, to put your energy toward turning things around and succeeding in this transition, then to assess honestly what *you* need to do to make it happen. You might reflect on whether you have changed enough to meet the new challenge. Consider if you have done enough to enable yourself to succeed—adapted your style, thought about your private goals and aspirations, gotten clear on what you're doing and why, or found meaning in the new position. Try the following:

- *Do some soul searching.* Ask yourself if this role connects to your core values and needs. Have you decided that this job is where you want to be and can commit yourself to continuing your transition? Once you resolve your own questions and know in your mind that you can and will successfully take on this challenge, you can move forward.
- *Decide how and where to get help.* You know you need to move forward and are trying to be successful in this role, but you also recognize that you can't do it alone. You know that you need additional help or support and are choosing to ask for it. For many people, choosing this option takes courage. Asking for help may require revealing where you are lacking and may be seen as a weakness by others. However, if you need to develop a particular skill, are missing some technical knowledge, need to develop more leadership experience, or haven't built a sufficient support network, then you need to get help.

Marshal assistance and get others more engaged to offer tips, teach you key skills, lend resources, or be a cheerleader. The best approach is to seek help sincerely and demonstrate that you are ready to receive it and act on it.

- *Be ready for feedback.* Learn to recognize feedback when you get it. Really listen and consider how you can act on it. You've probably already been receiving some feedback from others—comments offered after a meeting, questions they have asked, or even their facial expressions. Also, listen to your own internal feedback about what constitutes a job well done. The ability to give objective feedback to oneself is in fact the mark of the expert. (Csikszentmihalyi, 2003) Up to now, you may have focused only on the fact that the feedback hasn't been positive. Now that you have made a choice to make this work, consider how to use feedback to help you make progress.

The Decision to Exit This Transition

You may decide that, after giving your new role a reasonable try, it just isn't working out. First, don't assume that it's you who's fallen short. Recall Nigel from Chapter 3; his ultimate decision was that he really would be happier in a nonmanagement position. This transition may be proving too difficult for a reason–the new position may be a bad fit for you. Maybe it doesn't match what you love best, or maybe your personality doesn't mesh with the customer's. The person who recommended or selected you for the assignment may have been misinformed about the scope of the project and its associated demands. Perhaps you started out okay on this journey, but the terrain and surroundings (new objectives, new leaders) have changed since you initially said yes. Maybe the role itself is the problem—it doesn't fit in the organization's strategy, and whoever created it was mistaken in doing so. If the position or task is a mistake, there would be problems regardless of whom were to fill it. If for whatever reason there is a misalignment, you may decide to exit.

Be aware that choosing to exit this transition in itself implies beginning *another* transition. As you have been trying to work your way through this transition, the world around you has kept moving, and your previous role has likely changed as well. Imagine a flowing river; just as you cannot dip your toe in exactly the same river twice, you can't really return to your old job or team. Time didn't stand still while you were trying to work through this transition. Even if you have been gone only a short time, work situations have changed, and people have come and gone. Rather than thinking about going back to an old situation, think of yourself as moving forward to a new one—albeit one with which you have some familiarity.

Even those away for only a short time can find they need to transition back into that role when they return. One colleague relates that as part of her job, she would occasionally travel for several weeks at a time. She would frequently find that on returning to her role as mom, other family members had new routines, new preferences, or even new relationships. A few of her actions would provoke cries of, "Mom, we don't do it that way anymore!" She had to learn to integrate herself slowly into the new environment, rather than try to return to a state that no longer existed. Even within a few weeks time, she had changed, and so had they.

Not only do the details of a situation change, but so do the people and relationships. People will likely see you differently than they did before and, in turn, interact with you differently. Others may have no history with you, so new relationships must be established. At the same time, you may need to work through your own residual feelings about the halted transition. Some people have a hard time moving past a feeling of failure or frustration, even if it wasn't their fault that they couldn't continue in that new role.

A DECISION TO ADAPT AND MOVE FORWARD

Johanna, a successful corporate counsel, was instrumental in helping a company work through a very public and embarrassing situation that made the local headlines for months. She demonstrated perseverance, intelligence, good problem-solving skills, and an understanding of the perspectives of employees. As a result, she was offered the opportunity to head the human resources arm of one of the subsidiaries.

This job turned out to be very different than being a smart lawyer in a big law firm or even a corporate counsel. Johanna now had a staff of hundreds with responsibilities for critical functions that served employees (payroll, benefits, etc.) but tried to continue using her hands-on approach. In the first few months on the job, she nearly ran herself into an early grave, still trying to be the person who does the work rather than leading a very capable staff. She tried to be involved with every meeting and every decision to the point that she became physically ill. For the very first time in her life, problems were occurring on her watch. Although she didn't doubt her ability to do the job and wanted to remain, Johanna knew that she had to make some changes if she was going to turn things around, and she knew she needed help.

Following conversations with her boss and with peers who she respected, she recognized that a big part of the problem was her unwillingness to approach the job differently than the ones she had done before. Given the scope of her work, she needed to adjust her routines and behavior—to depend more on others, delegate work, and allow some decisions to move forward without her.

Johanna made two changes. First, she began changing her operating style. Instead of working one-on-one, she started getting her direct reports together to work in groups or as a team. Then, she found an external coach to help her better understand her own style and preferences and provide frank insights and advice on how she could use them to her advantage.

Over a period of a year, the challenges changed to successes—first small, then big. People started working together and being more effective on their own. Enabling them helped her. She regained her health and a big chunk of time she had been spending unproductively. Johanna now values her strength and identity as a leader who enables and supports the efforts of others. Since then, she has moved up further to a role in the global business and is poised for further progression to senior leadership.

A DECISION TO EXIT

Laura was facing a major crossroads in her life. She had been the executive director of a nonprofit in a small town for the past five years, had weathered a divorce three years ago, and was ready for change—even a move. She successfully interviewed for a job at a major university in a midsized town, four states away. Although she was not executive director at the new job, her experience and skills lent themselves well to the new position in development.

However, after the first three months, she knew she'd made a mistake. Not a mistake in the decision to leave her old job and find a new place to live—she'd exhausted the possibilities of the former job and had itched to get away from old memories. The mistake was not modifying her natural leadership abilities to fit her new job. Working with others, rather than having them work for her, was proving difficult. Laura lacked skill in influencing others and building consensus. Plus, she'd stepped on some toes early on while seeking information about big donors. "Don't even think about asking Mr. Smith for money—he's my prospect!" was just one of the responses to her queries.

Laura had sought advice from others in the department who she felt could help coach her along, and confided in one or two that she felt like she was failing. These feelings continued, and she had to make another major decision. At the six-month mark, she felt she could no longer make this job work, so she resigned to seek out other opportunities. Two months later, in a new position as an executive for another nonprofit, she reflected back on the experience and saw its value in helping her identify her core work values and ideal work environment.

WHAT TO DO

It's time to make a choice. Keep in mind, as with other parts of the transition process, you don't have to choose alone. We often can see ourselves reflected as we talk and interact with others. Use your network and support systems to figure out the best option for you and to help learn from your experience. Call your mentor or a trusted peer and explore your alternatives. Perhaps you got off to a rocky start but could still get on the right track.

If you choose to continue making the transition into this role, then:

- *Engage with others sooner rather than later.* Be proactive; a common mistake is waiting too long to ask for help. People get worried about their reputation or making a bad impression. So they delay; they fight it out alone and reinvent the wheel. Don't wait until you think you are ready; reach out for help early. It can be as simple as just asking for advice.

- *Ask for specific feedback.* Learn more about yourself through others, not just where you need to improve but how. Particularly in a transition, it's helpful to understand what is working and what isn't. Getting an outside opinion is important. You may be biased, being immersed in the new environment or situation, so a dispassionate observer can give you some perspective. Asking for feedback also is a way to extend an invitation to talk, providing an entry point to build a relationship.

- *Define and acknowledge the shift in your identity.* What does the new role imply for your routines—what you read, with whom you interact regularly, how you schedule your time, and what help you request? For example, some people who shift roles realize that they don't have time for all their household tasks and are at a stage where they can afford to hire someone else to mow their lawn or clean the house. Some may begin having lunch with a different set of people than before.

- *Set an incremental plan for change.* We often get so engrossed in a transition that we forget to step back, be reflective, and plan. Once you make a choice to continue in this transition and strive to be successful, don't expect immediate results. Take some time to understand what you've learned so far and how far you still have to go. Get some information on what's working and where you still need to adapt. Complete a simple gap analysis and then plan. What are your short-term goals? What are your long-term goals? What resources are missing? Who do you need to engage? What are potential obstacles?

- *Adjust the role.* Over time, you'll see what really needs to be done, which may be different than the original job description. (Hard to imagine, huh?) This is particularly true for a new position, where people were making a best guess about what the role would be like. You may need to define it once you have been in role for a few months. Some tasks will drop off while you pick up others. Depending on your staff, you may also adjust what you do versus what you assign to one of your team. At this stage, you may be able to recognize better what you need to keep and what your staff can comfortably take on.

If you decide to exit this transition and move on to something else, then:

- *Be really sure.* Avoid making emotional versus rational decisions because of your anxiety and the pressure of the current situation. In other words, don't just choose to remove the immediate pain of the situation. You could be sacrificing more in the long term, jeopardizing both your current role and future options.
- *Don't forget the transition pitfalls we've already discussed.* Moving on means starting a new transition. Don't say yes too quickly to another role in your haste to exit this situation. As the old saying goes, "The grass is always greener on the other side of the fence," especially when you are concentrating more on what you want to leave behind than on what you want to move toward. Consider why this role was a mismatch and try to avoid similar situations. Think about what would be a better fit for you and why. Set yourself up to succeed by focusing on moving toward what will work best for you rather than just focusing on how to move away from the current situation.
- *Be ready to tell your story.* People likely will ask about your latest change. Some will just be curious. Others will want more detail because in some way they have either been an active participant in your transition or were somehow affected by it. They want to understand the choice that you are making. How will you explain it to them?

- *Give yourself permission to be sad or disappointed.* Your emotions during this experience may have ranged from initial elation at the opportunity to real depression when you decided to call it quits. Even if logic says you have valid reasons for your decision—the job was a bad fit for you, the project was poorly defined, or the company had not thought through all of the implications of a new direction—allow yourself some time to work through your own personal disappointment when things don't work out as you'd hoped. Get support if you need it to work through the emotional toll of the experience. Talk to close friends or family, keep a journal, or take a short break between the two roles. Apply what you have learned from this experience to your next transition.

Whatever choices you make, build a support system to help with your efforts. As we've mentioned elsewhere in this book and in the entire *Leading from the Center* series, relationships are critical to your success as a manager. Whether you continue in the current transition or elect to transition elsewhere, you may need additional help. It may be support at work or in other domains of your life. By using your support system, you can continue your transition in a way that will help you succeed.

CHAPTER NINE

ON AUTOMATIC PILOT

TWO STEPS FORWARD, ONE STEP BACK

Congratulations! You made it through the toughest part of the curve! You've come a long way. You've experienced some of the traps, but you've gotten help from others, started to build some strong relationships, expanded your network, and made some choices about how to make this work. It's taken some time, but things are looking up. At this point, your routines are falling into place, and you've expanded your skills, adjusted your style, and are getting better at the new challenges you've taken on. Slowly, you have achieved a set of small wins. Your new role doesn't feel as new or as difficult as it once did, and you're feeling better about your ability to succeed. In some ways, you've acted your way into a new way of thinking, shifting a couple of key beliefs along the way. Across multiple layers of your identity, you have added dimension to who you are, making you better prepared for the next challenge.

If you think it's a smooth path from this point forward, then you may fall into the final trap—**thinking you are all set.** Even if you feel you've made the right choice, this final zone can be a little rocky as you go through the process of trial and error in figuring out its implementation. The danger here is of getting too comfortable too quickly. Rather than a clean progression from choice to transformation, your movement is more likely to be a series of stops and starts, progress and regression, small wins and small setbacks. Don't consider two steps forward as a guarantee of success, but neither should you consider one step backward as a sign of failure. Expect a mixture of both as you work your way forward.

As you continue to learn, grow, and develop in your new identity, your forward progress will outweigh the missteps. Keep searching for ways to be more effective, to learn new skills or information, to check in regularly with others to get feedback, and to make adjustments as needed. Those who don't commit to continuous growth can easily become misaligned or lose energy and momentum.

A PAUSE ALONG THE JOURNEY

If you rest, you rust.
Helen Hayes

In time, the process really does begin to feel complete. Projects are moving along on schedule, your own growth is on target, and you and your team can largely run on automatic pilot. You can sit back, rest on your accomplishments, and just keep doing more of what you're doing, right? Not quite.

Instead of celebrating this as your final destination, consider it a milestone along a longer but as yet unknown journey. All life is like a never-ending experiment, one that carries with it a guarantee that change will happen. The degree of change may lessen, but it doesn't go away entirely. This isn't the end, so keep looking to the future.

You should always strive to be better even in your current role, to be open to new ideas and approaches, and to stay up-to-date in your field and in your organization. Managers in the center of the organization often take lateral moves; the skills you develop with this transition are likely to serve you well for several years and a few more transitions. Becoming excellent in this role is worth your effort.

Consider Tyler, a successful line vice president for a manufacturing company. He had spent the first dozen years of his career as a management consultant before moving to his VP position. He wanted to "do" instead of offer advice to others, and running a small piece of a big business was just what he wanted. Being new to the company, as he became more comfortable in the role, he set out to build broad networks and learn as much as he could about the business beyond his own area. When the company was looking to expand, they approached Tyler—did he want to stay where he was, go run a small niche business the company just bought 175 miles away, or move to Asia where they were going to open a new factory? By becoming excellent at his current role, he had earned the opportunity to take on a similar role with a broader scope or in a new culture. By making connections with others, he also extended others' awareness of his capabilities and readiness. And because the new challenges built on his existing abilities, he had a higher probability of success.

Consider what's next for you, your goals and aspirations, and what you might do now that will make that next transition smoother. Underestimating the likelihood and impact of the next role change can make that next transition more difficult than it needs to be. If you think you're all set, you may be focusing on the wrong things or not preparing for your next challenge as well as you could. For example, a star individual contributor spent her first year learning about her new company and building experience and expertise in the organization's products and services. She was so focused on transitioning well into becoming an individual contributor that she didn't start preparing to lead a team, the next step in the company's career progression. When confronted with the promotion, she was ill-prepared to take it. She hadn't looked ahead.

Just when you're getting comfortable, it may be hard to think of jumping back into the uncertainty of more changes, but this probably is *not* the last opportunity you will have. More transitions are coming down the road. Some will appear unexpectedly, while you may have been anticipating or even pursuing others. When opportunities for a change in role do occur, remember the transition zones and pitfalls but also the multiple layers of identity change that may be part of your transition. You may have to work through change at several levels of your identity before reaching the zone of Confidence and Transformation.

WHAT TO DO

Celebrate, Renew, and Recover

In today's world, the frequency of transitions can feel exhausting. We can get so caught up in the process of working our way through new or changing roles, projects, teams, skills, and knowledge that we don't recognize the amount of energy and effort the process has taken. Take some time to celebrate the journey you have just navigated and renew your spirit and energy. Recognize and celebrate not just your own accomplishments but also the efforts of all of those who have helped and supported you. As we mentioned earlier, no one goes through this alone. Many people have been going through their own transition process in parallel to yours. With renewed energy, you and others are better able to reflect and look forward to the next learning or growth opportunity with enthusiasm.

Reflect on What's Going Well and Build on It

Now that you have succeeded in the major shifts, you can focus on nuance. You have become competent in most aspects of your role. At this point, you might think about which areas you want to become expert in. Talking with those in your network and looking at trends in the company or marketplace can help you determine what skills, experience, or knowledge are particularly valuable. You might consider how to develop yourself in those particular areas. Getting feedback from others is an important step.

After deciding where to focus attention, think about how you can get coaching to improve. Who has this expertise? What can you learn from that person?

You can also focus on getting your team working more smoothly or efficiently. For example, you might see if there are processes that you can modify, now that you understand how they work. Check that your team has effective routines for the work they're doing. In monitoring the environment, you might learn of a talented person elsewhere in the organization who could help your team.

Pay Attention

Once you are comfortable in your role, make sure that you're paying attention to all of the challenges of today's manager that we describe throughout the *Leading from the Center* series. Are your goals and objectives aligned with the larger strategy? Is your team or project well aligned with other groups, divisions, or initiatives? Turn some attention to monitoring the environment. Which way is the political wind blowing? As we've discussed elsewhere, effective managers gain by collaborating with others. They look for opportunities to experiment, innovate, and build the future. They help those around them understand what to do and why.

All of these tasks are important. And all require being aware of and engaged in your organization. In the midst of a transition, you may not have the attention span to do this well, being so focused on your immediate problems. However, once you are more settled, make sure that you are aligning with all of the aspects of your role.

Be Open to Ideas or Suggestions

Feeling like you have successfully transitioned to a new role doesn't mean that everything is going as well as it could. Now that you have a handle on the day-to-day rhythm, you can turn your attention to how your routines *could* go. You may want to consider an employee's idea on how to reorganize the forms, or process orders faster, or some other aspect of your work. You have some personal momentum now as well as the support of others. This is the perfect time to push on to achieve even better performance.

We say that in the center of the organization people need to manage today, with an eye toward the future. That advice holds for your career path, too. Consider where you would like to go next.

What options hold the most appeal, and what steps do you need to take to prepare for them? Recall the guiding principles that we put forth in Chapter 2, and continue to rely on them. First, it's likely that the transition isn't really complete; and second, the principles are as useful during periods of calm and stability as during periods of extreme change. Continue to be aware, curious, and forward-looking. Continue to believe you have something to learn and new dimensions to your identity to discover and develop. Continue to connect with others along the way, and continue to invest in your own development because it's an ongoing process.

When the next opportunity to say "Yes!" occurs, you'll be ready.

BIBLIOGRAPHY

Bridges, William. 2003. *Managing Transitions: Making the Most of Change*, 2nd ed. Cambridge, Mass: Da Capo Press.

Charan, Ram, Stephen Drotter, and James Noel. 2000. *The Leadership Pipeline: How to Build the Leadership-Powered Company*. San Francisco: Jossey-Bass, Inc.

Ciampa, Dan, and Michael Watkins. 1999. *Right from the Start: Taking Charge in a New Leadership Role*. Boston: Harvard Business School Press.

Csikszentmihalyi, Mihaly. 2003. *Good Business: Leadership, Flow, and the Making of Meaning*. New York City: Penguin Putnam, Inc.

Dotlich, David L., James L. Noel, and Normal Walker. 2004. *Leadership Passages: The Personal and Professional Transitions That Make or Break a Leader*. San Francisco: John Wiley and Sons, Inc.

Drucker, Peter F. 2002. *The Effective Executive*. New York City: HarperCollins Publishers, Inc.

Grant, Anne, Ph.D. 1997. *Suggestions for Coping with Grief*. San Francisco: KAIROS Support for Caregivers.

Hayes, Helen. 1990. *My Life in Three Acts*. New York City: Harcourt.

Hill, Linda. 2003. *Becoming a Manager: How New Managers Master the Challenges of Leadership*. Boston: Harvard Business School Press.

Hopson, Barrie, and John Adams. 1976. *Transition: Understanding and Managing Personal Change*. London: Martin Robertson.

Johnson, Lauren Keller. 2005. "The New Loyalty: Make It Work for Your Company." *Harvard Management Update* 10(3) 3–5 (March 2005).

Joni, Sai-nicole. 2004. *The Third Opinion*. New York City: Penguin Group (USA), Inc.

Keegan, Robert. 1994. *In Over Our Heads: The Mental Demands of Modern Life*. Boston: Harvard University Press.

Lohr, Steve. "Can This Man Reprogram Microsoft?" *New York Times*. Sunday, 11 December 2005. Business section: 1, 4.

McCormick, Blaine. 2001. *At Work with Thomas Edison: Ten Business Lessons from America's Greatest Innovator*. Canada: Entrepreneur Press.

United States Department of Labor, Bureau of Labor Statistics. 2002. "Number of Jobs Held, Labor Market Activity, and Earnings Growth among Younger Baby Boomers." 27 August 2002.

Watkins, Michael. 2003. *The First 90 Days*. Boston: Harvard Business School Publishing.

—— 2001. *Taking Charge in Your New Leadership Role: A Workbook*. Boston: Harvard Business School Press.

Williams, Dai. 1999. "Life Events and Career Change: Transition Psychology in Practice" (*www.eoslifework.co.uk/transprac.htm*). Paper presented to the British Psychological Society's Occupational Psychology Conference, January.

INDEX